RENEWALS 458-4574

THE EMPOWERMENT COOKBOOK

Action Plans for Creating, Sustaining or Refocusing Empowered Work Teams

RUSSELL D. ROBINSON

McGraw-Hill
New York San Francisco Washington, D.C. Auckland Bogotá
Caracas Lisbon London Madrid Mexico City Milan
Montreal New Delhi San Juan Singapore
Sydney Tokyo Toronto

To all of us who seek a better way . . . especially those change agents worldwide who see the importance of having a vision and dedicate themselves to making it a reality.

Library of Congress Cataloging-in-Publication Data

Robinson, Russell D.
    The empowerment cookbook : action plans for creating, sustaining, or refocusing empowered work teams / Russell D. Robinson.
      p.   cm.
    Includes index.
    ISBN 0-7863-1193-2
    1. Employee empowerment.   2. Industrial management—Employee participation.   3. Work groups.   I. Title.
HD50.5.R63   1997   96-47631
658.4'02—dc21
http: www.mhcollege.com

McGraw-Hill

A Division of The **McGraw·Hill** Companies

Copyright © 1997 by Russell D. Robinson. All rights reserved. Printed in the United States of America. Except as permitted under the United States Copyright Act of 1976, no part of this publication may be reproduced or distributed in any form or by any means, or stored in a database or retrieval system, without the prior written permission of the copyright holder.

1 2 3 4 5 6 7 8 9 0DOC/DOC9 0 9 8 7 6

ISBN 0-7863-1193-2

Printed and bound by R.R. Donnelley & Sons Company.

This publication is designed to provide accurate and authoritative information in regard to the subject matter covered. It is sold with the understanding that neither the author nor the publisher is engaged in rendering legal, accounting, or other professional service. If legal advice or other expert assistance is required, the services of a competent professional person should be sought.
                              —*From a Declaration of Principles jointly adopted by a committee*
                                of the American Bar Association and a Committee of Publishers.

McGraw-Hill books are available at special quantity discounts to use as premiums and sales promotions, or for use in corporate training programs. For more information, please write to the Director of Special Sales, McGraw-Hill, 11 West 19th Street, New York, NY 10011. Or contact your local bookstore.

The Empowerment Cookbook Process Model

Organization Temperature

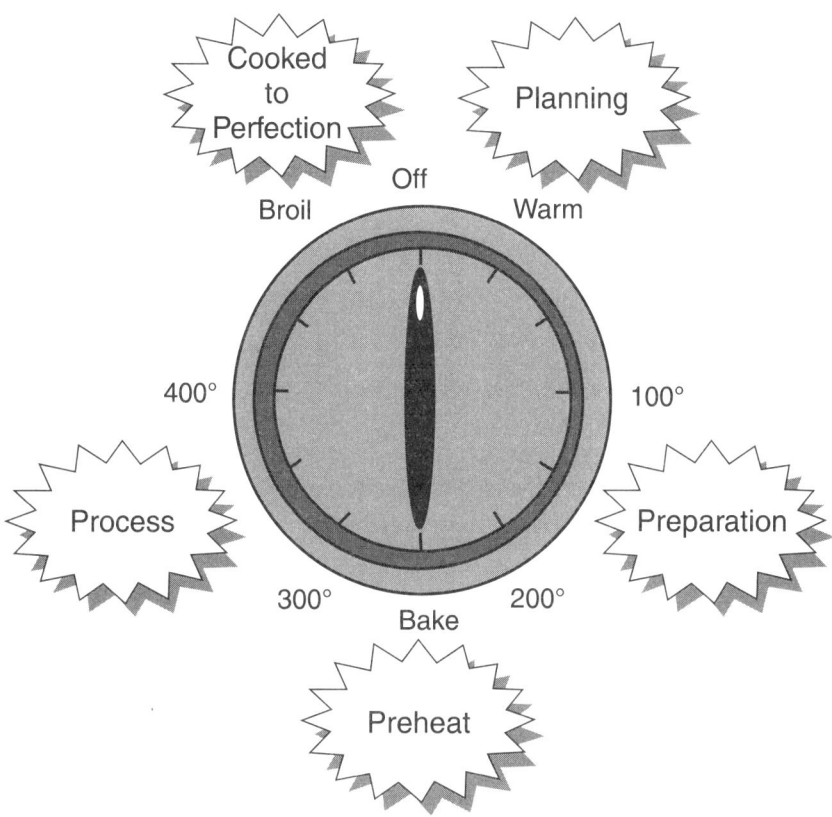

MENU

PART ONE
PLANNING
Recipes

Planning 3
Current State Assessment 5
    Sample Current State Assessment Survey 5
    Sample Cover Letter 7
    Sample Distribution 9
Design Team Formation 10
As-Is Process Map 17
    Sample Process Map Disconnects 19
Future State Vision 20
Summary 24

PART TWO
PREPARATION
Recipes

Preparation 27
Mission 28
    Sample Mission 29
Objectives Matrix 30
    Sample Objectives Matrix 31
Skills Inventory 35
Goals 38
    Sample Goals 40
Should-Be Process Map 41
Summary 45

PART THREE
PREHEAT
Recipes

Preheat 49

Menu　　　　　　　　　　　　　　　　　　　　　　　　　　v

Flash Meeting   51
Cross-Training Matrix   55
Co-Location   59
Functional Parity   61
Benchmarking   63
Customer Visits   65
Summary   70

PART FOUR

PROCESS

Recipes

Process   73
Communication Strategy   75
Job Redesign   78
Information Sharing   81
Team-Based Pay/Recognition   83
Reward and Recognition   87
　　Sample Reward and Recognition   89
Summary   92

PART FIVE

COOKED TO PERFECTION

Recipes

Cooked to Perfection   97
Transition   99
Alignment   101
Partnership   104
Renewal   107
Summary   111

PART SIX

DESSERT

Recipe

Dessert   115
Empowermints   116
Epilogue   118
　　Issues in Implementing Empowered Teams   118

PREFACE

After countless starts, endless excuses, and infinite rewrites, I am convinced that the most difficult aspect of writing a book is having patience. Especially for this novice, who previously had never ventured into anything beyond a lengthy term paper or fact-filled memo. There were moments when the will to conquer this process seemed nonexistent, but success can be a powerful catalyst!

Although I am not formally recognized as such, I have considered myself to be a CEO, for a major global corporation, for a considerable length of time. As you would expect, a lack of that formal recognition has had its drawbacks. Nevertheless, like its formal counterpart, it is a role of leadership and vision, entrusted with creating a competitive advantage. It is a role where resiliency and a passion for change are prerequisites for success. It is a role where modeling expected behaviors will generate support and motivation for a desired outcome. It is, for all practical purposes, a critical position in organizations bold enough to explore new frontiers of performance and reshape organizational culture. As you might guess, I am not the Chief Executive Officer, but rather a Champion of Empowered Organizations!

At this juncture of my career, I am not a consultant; I am still a practitioner and strategist, with a passion and desire to leverage employee involvement and the empowerment concept as a competitive advantage. I have survived a long tenure in a leadership role within manufacturing, championing strategic change efforts. I have also undertaken a similar effort in the nonmanufacturing ranks, which has posed a new set of challenges. Although a majority of empowered team implementations have occurred within manufacturing, the same competitive pressures exist on the professional side. Flatter and leaner organizations, rapidly changing technology, and the demand for speed precipitate the need for greater employee involvement and empowerment. My experience has been that although the appearance, structure, and motivations may be different, the continued growth of empowered teams in the nonmanufacturing segment will continue to accelerate and flourish.

Preface

The empowerment concept has been driven to the forefront as an evolutionary process for improving business performance. Using numerous acronyms like SMTs (self-managed teams) and HPWTs (high-performance work teams), a significant number of publications have identified empowerment as a breakthrough opportunity for strategic leverage, and rightfully so!

As Champions of Empowered Organizations, you will control an exhaustive menu of change drivers that can foster the empowerment initiative. However, a successful change process can be elusive. The transition can be stressful. As critical an element of business success as empowerment is, my experience is that the staffing of this role is minimal, with organizational responsibility sometimes at question. Yet, the expectation of this role is to lead, coach, and facilitate organizations to a successful transition from the status quo to a future vision. Champions seeking direction, clarification, or alternatives for a change strategy have only a few sources that provide useful information.

The intent of this book was to provide a concept resource guide for champions that have a vision beyond the status quo and a sense of urgency to make the journey. Thus, I was determined to create a book format that the reader could engage frequently for quick reference. As I thought about what would accomplish that objective, I realized that it already existed: a cookbook. Because it focuses on the end result (output), the ingredients (input), and the how-to steps (process), the cookbook approach seemed an ideal match. In fact, when I recalled the number of times I heard the remark "There is no cookbook for empowerment," the concept choice became obvious!

The Empowerment Cookbook is designed in a format useful for a diverse audience. It is filled with recipes for creating, sustaining, or refocusing the empowerment initiative in any type of business. This book is based on what I have learned from years of practical experience and benchmarking. For executives, middle managers, and support staff responsible for bringing the potential of a team vision to reality and creating a competitive advantage, this book will provide a process to accomplish those goals. For facilitators, consultants, trainers, front line supervision, and change agents with direct responsibility to champion a team strategy, this book will be invaluable as a how-to guide and tool set. For steering committees and design teams chartered with creating and enabling a change process for team evolution, this book details the steps needed in shaping a new vision and culture. Finally, team members will also benefit from reading *The Empowerment Cookbook*—it will provide a framework for organizational change and stimulate their thinking about the linkage between teamwork and performance improvement.

Finally, I believe it is important, when evolving an empowered team strategy, to highlight the fact that there are subtle differences between manufacturing and nonmanufacturing business segments. As a practitioner and champion in both arenas, I have learned to make that distinction and engage a different set of actions or tools to facilitate change. Therefore, each recipe in this book indicates whether the "serving" should be strictly for manufacturing or non-manufacturing or should be for both. Chapter-closing models reinforce any differences in recipes for each of the two business segments, and the recipes should be prepared and served in the sequence indicated at each process stage.

The Empowerment Cookbook begins with a prologue that defines the context of empowerment and describes the key features of empowered teams. Empowerment as a change strategy is a response to change drivers that present a compelling case for change, and several critical change drivers are highlighted here. Finally, teams will transition through multiple stages of evolution along an empowerment continuum, and each of these stages is characterized by the changing roles of managers and members alike. Entry points along the empowerment continuum for application of the elements of *The Empowerment Cookbook* process model are also highlighted.

Part One focuses on the planning element of *The Empowerment Cookbook* process model. Planning recipes provide the steps necessary to ready the organization for an empowered team strategy.

Part Two presents the preparation element of *The Empowerment Cookbook* process model. Preparation recipes describe the steps necessary to launch an empowered team initiative.

Part Three is the preheat element of *The Empowerment Cookbook* process model. Preheat recipes continue to warm the organization to the concept of empowerment and provide the catalyst for increasing the level of involvement and interaction among team members.

Part Four offers the process element of *The Empowerment Cookbook* model. Process recipes serve the organization with the steps that are essential to evolve a team-based paradigm shift.

Part Five deals with the cooked-to-perfection element of *The Empowerment Cookbook* process model. Cooked-to-perfection recipes position the organization to complete a successful transition to empowered teams and to sustain the change.

Part Six celebrates a successful outcome to the empowered team initiative and offers a recipe for dessert that will have you tasting success.

The Empowerment Cookbook closes with the epilogue that identifies several issues to consider when implementing empowered teams. This section details the critical need to build a compelling case for change to secure sponsorship. It highlights the pace of each team's change effort and the subsequent process time to effect a successful transition. It also discusses the types of champions and their consequences in a change effort, and touches on legal issues and the role of organized labor. Lastly, it offers some thoughts on the future of empowered teams.

Finally, as you turn these pages, look for the step-saving tips designed to speed up empowerment preparation time. Every recipe has been carefully developed and tested to ensure the intended results. For quick fixes or appetizers, select only those recipes that will satisfy a specific customer expectation. In organizations where you have a little more time, consider using all of the entrees.

I strongly believe that empowerment is that breakthrough opportunity for all businesses to leverage in improving business performance. I hope that you will benefit from this book, as you successfully implement the empowerment initiative in your organizations. As <u>C</u>hampions of <u>E</u>mpowered <u>O</u>rganizations, take pride while your organizations cook to perfection!

Russell D. Robinson

ACKNOWLEDGMENTS

I realized long before this book was completed that a significant number of people past and present have contributed to or influenced this book's reality. I will forever be indebted for the experiences, the intellectual exchange, and the innovation for all who collaborated in change strategies as partners and friends.

First and foremost, I would like to thank Motorola for being world-class in everything they do. The reasons for being leading edge are countless. I will never forget those individuals and teams who listened, suggested, reacted, and changed the status quo. They are the real heroes in a change process and the influence for this book.

Sponsorship is a critical element of any change process, and I am grateful to those leaders who had the courage and foresight to embrace a vision. My thanks to Kim Fudge and Rick MacDonald, at Motorola, for their encouragement and resolve, and to a multitude of others who believed or became believers.

My love and thanks to my daughter Kristen, who for the six years of her life has taught me so many things and made life less complex and more fun. There is a simplicity to her years that keeps life in perspective; may it always remain so.

My family has always been there for support in whatever road I have journeyed. To my mom, brother, aunt, and niece, my love and thanks. To my late father, whose values, friendship, and counsel were invaluable, he is missed.

A special thanks to Jeffrey Krames, Cindy Zigmund, and the team at Irwin Professional Publishing for giving me an opportunity to be an author; a thought and a dream became a reality.

Having friends who encourage, challenge, and listen has been an integral part of my life. Continued friendship and thanks to Candy Matheson, Michelle Bradtke, Bob Carroll, Rosemary Kiekow, Linda Rodina, Raymond Massie, Rosa Rhodes, Aleta Shasteen, Jeanne Stoner, and Liz Johnson. Everyone should be as fortunate as I am.

A special thanks to Diane Landry for her unwavering confidence, support, and inspiration. I don't know if I would have stayed the course without her.

I would especially like to thank those who helped with specific feedback about the book. My thanks to Liz Johnson, of SDA Corporation; Linda Rodina at Motorola; Janet Malloy, of Innovative Leadership Technologies; and Abe Raab, of The Alexander Graham Raab Consulting Group.

I am indebted to all of you for your encouragement, friendship, patience, and support.

ABOUT THE AUTHOR

Russell D. Robinson is the manager of Sector Empowerment Initiatives, Land Mobile Products Sector, Motorola, Schaumburg, Illinois. He received his B.S. degree (1973) in operations management from Northern Illinois University, DeKalb, Illinois.

As a twenty-one year Motorolan, Russ has spent his career concentrated in materials and manufacturing management, and most recently in human resources as an internal consultant/facilitator driving the empowerment initiative in the nonmanufacturing segment of the business. Russ has presented at numerous private- and public-sector conferences relative to the implementation of high-performance/empowered teams.

PROLOGUE

The factors that frame today's success will often create tomorrow's failure. It has been my experience that success conditions many organizations to continue old ways of doing business. However, there is a high probability that past practices will not ensure future success and, in fact, will constrain an organization's progress. It seems a foregone conclusion that failure to react quickly to remain competitive in today's global environment places survival in a tenuous position. Business as usual must be viewed as totally unacceptable. Business has to change to survive!

Many experts have addressed the issue of how to create change. The common thread running through the successful application of change strategies is the involvement of many employees in crafting a vision and embracing the journey. The key is to encourage employees to take initiative and to become more involved in the success or failure of the enterprise. The process for securing that involvement and creating change is empowerment.

WHAT IS EMPOWERMENT?

It is becoming increasingly apparent that the major source of competitive advantage lies in the dedication, creativity, and energy of employees. Empowerment is the catalyst that fuels a changing workplace. People want to make a difference and organizations desperately need them to. Yet, organizations have difficulty in harnessing employee capability and energy.

So what is empowerment? Empowerment is a process that will enhance effectiveness and business performance. It is a process that will bring about significant changes in an organization's culture and climate. It is a process that maximizes the utilization of the different capabilities of members. Empowerment focuses on changing the cultural fabric of an organization. It is an evolution of behaviors and mindset that transcends organizational structures and reporting relationships.

A definition that I believe captures the essence of empowerment within an organization is that of "a strategic process of building a partnership between people and the organization, fostering trust, responsibility, authority and accountability to best serve the customer."

"Empowerment for all, in a Participative, Cooperative and Creative Workplace..." is one of Motorola's key corporate initiatives.

WHAT IS AN EMPOWERED TEAM?

Whereas a traditional work group is generally organized into separate specialized jobs with narrow responsibilities, an empowered team is a natural work group of employees who are responsible and accountable for a whole work process, product, or service. Typically, empowered teams share leadership; collaborate to continuously improve their work processes; plan and make decisions relative to methods of work, priorities, and assignments; and resolve problematic issues. Some of the key features of empowered teams are:

- ✔Various leadership and administrative tasks are shared.
- ✔Members have the ability to evaluate and improve the quality of information processes and performance.
- ✔The team provides inputs to business strategy.
- ✔Commitment, flexibility, and creativity are fundamental to achieving organization/team goals.
- ✔There is cultural sensitivity in a diverse workplace and world.
- ✔Empowered teams coordinate and interface with other teams/organizations.
- ✔There is enhanced honesty and trust in communications and relationships.
- ✔Empowered teams display enthusiasm and a positive attitude.

Empowered teams are not the solution for every organization's current and future needs. They will not resolve every problem nor address every performance challenge. Empowered teams, however, do represent one of the best ways to support changes that are necessary for a high-performing enterprise.

The table below illustrates the contrast between traditional organizations and empowered team organizations.

Elements of Cultural Change

Element	Traditional	Empowered Team
People culture	Controlled/centralized	Trust/delegation/risk
View of the employee	Employee as a cost	Employee as an asset
Work organization	Specialized/functional	Teams/cross-functional
Structure	Layered/autocratic	Flat/participative
Corporate culture	Rigid/bureaucratic	Adaptive/supportive
Employee knowledge	Need to know	Broad
Job design	Narrow/single task	Whole process/multiple task
Skills training	Technical	Technical and social
Change	Resist	Embrace
Rate of change	Slow	Rapid
Management role	Direct/control/manage	Coach/facilitate/lead
Decision making	Chain-of-command	Diffused
Rewards	Individual/seniority	Team-based/multidimensional
Information flow	Limited	Shared
Employee autonomy	Low	High

FACTORS FOR CHANGE

Change has always been a management challenge, but what is different today is the magnitude of change that companies are encountering. The kinds of broadbased changes that confront organizations today require that a significant number of employees exhibit new and untested behaviors and skills. Many firms will not succeed without participation and a shared sense of direction by people throughout the organization. This process is driven by recognizing or anticipating change drivers, which are the internal or external forces that compel an organization to change. I have experienced or benchmarked the following change drivers:

- ✔ Accelerated global competition.
- ✔ Dissatisfied customers.
- ✔ Slow speed of product innovation and introduction.
- ✔ Flatter and leaner organizations.
- ✔ Bureaucratic infighting and inertia.
- ✔ Rapidly changing technology.
- ✔ Changing worker values.
- ✔ Productivity/efficiency stagnation.

Prologue

As a champion, you will not have to look hard for change drivers—I guarantee they will find you! Realize that your success will be measured in terms of your response to these compelling needs.

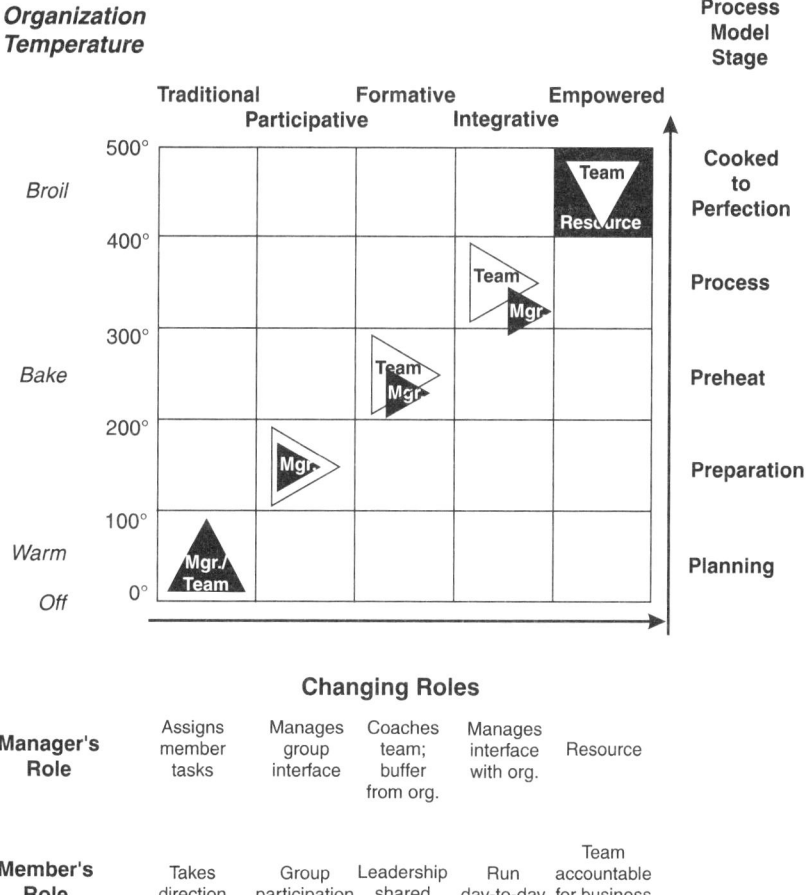

As teams progress along the empowerment continuum (on page xviii), leadership and managerial responsibilities shift to the team. In the traditional stage, the top down hierarchical structure (depicted by a triangle) signifies an autocratic workplace, with management (shaded area) having undisputed influence and authority over team members. Management assigns each member's tasks, and each member's role is that of taking direction. This is the structural relationship of most organizations today. The traditional stage in the continuum of empowered team evolution obviously provides fertile ground for the planning element of *The Empowerment Cookbook* process model.

In the participative stage, the manager is still the focal point for group dynamics in terms of facilitating activities and performance. However, the downward transformation of leadership begins at this stage, with the manager starting to share some control and problem-solving activities with group members. Member participation in some of the shared leadership and problem-solving activities becomes the first step in an evolutionary process of increasing the level of member involvement. The rotation of the triangle (representing the team) signifies a slight transformation of the traditional top down structure as the manager begins to share some responsibility (reduced shaded area within the triangle) and slightly decreases the range of influence or authority over the team. The preparation element of *The Empowerment Cookbook* process model has application for this stage of transition.

The formative stage marks the formation of teams as crossfunctional training begins. This stage is highlighted by extended shared leadership between the manager and the team. The manager's role becomes one of coaching and coordinating group skills, activities, and performance, while serving as a buffer between the hierarchy of the organization and the team. The manager in this stage may also militate toward exploring more strategic organizational issues, as the capability and capacity of the team increases. Shared leadership with team members becomes a function of member cross-training in technical and administrative areas and coaching in performance improvement and leadership activities. The triangle remains in the same rotated state, with the manager's influence or authority (shaded area) transitioning to a coaching role within the team and migrating somewhat outside the scope of the team for involvement in more broad organizational issues. The preheat element of *The Empowerment Cookbook* process model provides the transition to this stage.

In the integrative stage, the manager has less contact with individual team members, but is still responsible for overall team performance. The manager evaluates performance data and provides diagnostic support and feedback for corrective action, as necessary. A significant aspect of the manager's role is to interface with the organization and other teams. Individual team member roles and skills are formally integrated into the team to optimize team performance, as the team assumes responsibility for daily activities, problem solving, and response. The team triangle remains in the same rotated state, with the manager's influence or authority over the team continuing to decrease and shift outside of the team's scope. The process element of *The Empowerment Cookbook* model promotes the redistribution of responsibility and transition to this stage.

Achieving empowerment is the fifth and final stage of team evolution. The empowered team is accountable for its total business performance and no longer depends on the manager. With redistribution of responsibility complete, the manager's role is now that of a team resource available for consultation as required. At this stage, the manager's time and effort is absorbed by the larger organization. This transformation is depicted by the inverted triangle signifying that the structure is no longer top-down, but rather an inverse of the traditional organizational structure. The cooked-to-perfection element of *The Empowerment Cookbook* process model assists in completing this transition and sustaining this state of change.

There is also a significant difficulty in the downward transformation of leadership responsibilities. The changing roles of managers and team members as the evolution to team empowerment proceeds can cause considerable role confusion for everyone concerned. It is therefore important to define roles clearly before and during the transformation process. Even so, change takes time.

It has been my experience that it will take a team or organization approximately fifteen months to five years to evolve through these five stages. A high level of sponsorship, commitment, and support will hasten the journey; so, as a champion, keep turning the heat up!

RESULTS

Having developed, coached, and facilitated a significant number of teams in both the manufacturing and nonmanufacturing arenas, I can guarantee that the opportunity for increasing performance is too great not to make the effort and investment. Improved business performance is the name of the game! A results mentality will not only speed the pace of transformation, but will sustain the momentum, harness new supporters, and indoctrinate the rest of the organization to a better way of addressing the broad-based changes necessary for survival.

On the manufacturing side, I have personally experienced the energy and enthusiasm as teams have improved quality, cycle time, productivity, and safety. I have seen employees become revitalized by having a voice in decision making, sharing leadership, making process improvements, and redesigning jobs and systems. Their personal growth has been remarkable and a factor in their continued commitment to the empowerment process and change strategy.

On the nonmanufacturing side, results have been equally impressive in many of the same areas. Improvements in time to market, cost reductions, cross-functional support, and customer/supplier interface has improved dramatically.

For all practical purposes, I think it would be premature to try to prove the value of team empowerment by citing upward trends in familiar business statistics. In an important sense, we've only just begun. These teams are still evolving and performance is still escalating. Until I actually became involved in team strategy, I did not appreciate the potential they represent. If you are unpersuaded—even skeptical—about team value, I urge you to challenge such notions by benchmarking and seeing teams in action. I have become convinced that every business or organization faces performance challenges for which teams are the most practical and powerful solution. Indeed, the best thing about teams is that they make a difference!

PART ONE

PLANNING

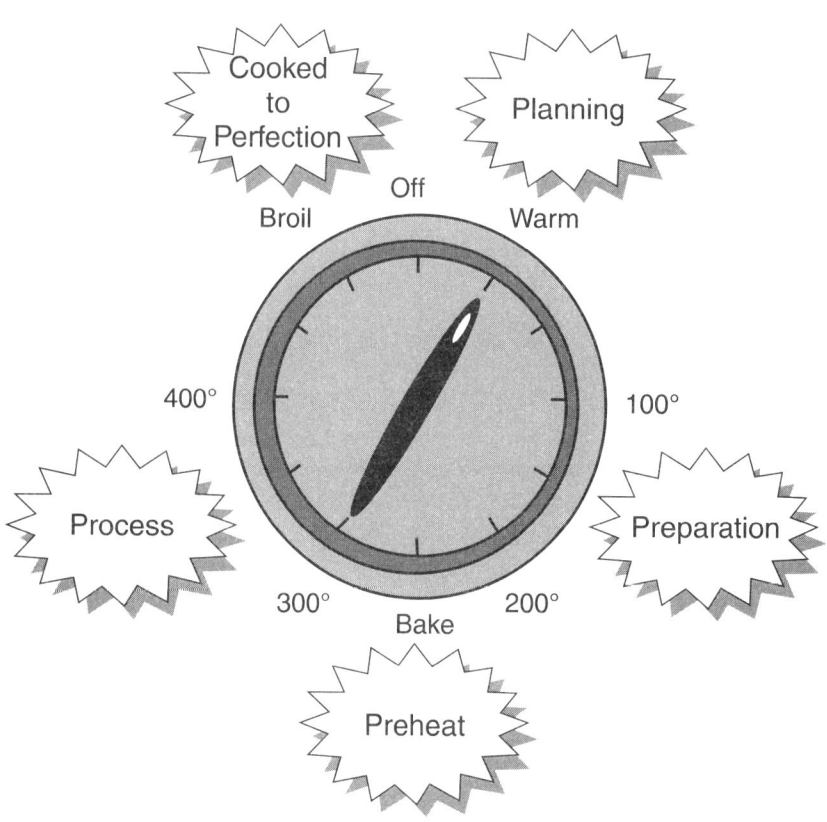

PLANNING

Recipe collections in this part of the book begin the planning process for the implementation of empowered teams. Before you begin, read through a recipe for a thorough understanding of ingredients, templates, and techniques. Clear how-to directions and samples will acquaint you with some of the more essential empowerment-planning tools. Whether you're a novice or a seasoned champion, you'll enjoy making the recipes in this planning collection!

✳ Planning begins when a champion formulates a current state assessment survey that will elicit responses as to the perceived current state of the organization or team. The existing culture, effectiveness and compatibility of operating systems, and performance challenges will signal the appropriateness, timing, and prospects for embracing a change strategy.

Assuming that the current state assessment has yielded the need and urgency for change, the champion takes the next step in the planning process: formation of a design team chartered with designing, implementing, and monitoring progress along the empowerment continuum. Design team members must be carefully selected—they will serve the organization a strategy of their creation or influence.

✳ The next step in the empowerment-planning process is developing and completing an environmental scan, an analysis of who interfaces with an organization or team and their expectations. For a change of pace from the classic scan, blend in the empowered team's expectations for each environmental interface. For added zip, indicate which of the respective needs are not being met.

Assessing the level of empowerment sponsorship of key stakeholders follows the completion of the environmental scan. It is important to have sponsors believe in the long term impact that empowerment will have on the organization, so that they will display public support, provide resources, change business systems, and advocate the change strategy. Actions that are intended to shift selected stakeholders to new sponsorship levels are identified and carried out. In fact, information derived from the current state assessment and the environmental scan will add flavor as discussion points with stakeholders.

Completing the as-is process map representing the organization's or team's conversion process is the next step in the planning process. Beginning the journey is difficult if you don't know where the starting point is!

Finally, creating a shared vision of a new tomorrow becomes the enticement for change. The challenge is when the new tomorrow is drastically different from the path of experience.

You are now ready to select the planning recipes that will begin the empowerment journey. Samples of some of the featured entrees are included for you to savor. Plan well—change is imminent!

CURRENT STATE ASSESSMENT

For a no-fuss, keep-cool appetizer, serve an assortment of questions that will elicit responses about the current state of the organization or team.

Ingredients:
   1 packet condensed survey questions
   1 cover letter
   1 distribution list

Makes one serving (for manufacturing or nonmanufacturing)

1. In a small-to-medium questionnaire (one-three pages) mix in questions relative to strategy, organizational structure, systems, skills, management style, and shared values.
2. Serve topped with a cover letter stating the intent of the survey and the date when a summary of responses will be analyzed and distributed.
3. Combine all responses; blend common themes and sort statements that are not related.
4. Add summary and distribute.

Variation
Substitute appropriate external consultant surveys (if desired) for internally designed survey packet. Two consulting firms with experience and supporting materials in the area of empowered or high-performance work teams are Development Dimensions International, headquartered in Pittsburgh, Pennsylvania, and Zenger-Miller, Inc., based in San Jose, California.

Tip
For best results, season with commentary relative to the next step in the formation of a design team and the prospects for a change strategy.

Sample Current State Assessment Survey

Strategy
   1. What is the current business strategy?

2. What elements of the business (e.g., product portfolio/markets/performance/people) does the strategy incorporate?
3. What time frame does the business strategy cover?
4. How do we diversify and develop our workforce for competitive advantage?
5. What are the critical, unique strategic advantages/core competencies of the business/organization that must be leveraged and capitalized on?
6. What is the strategy to perform necessary work with fewer resources?
7. What products and/or services must be added to the portfolio to meet customer expectations and attract new business?

Structure

1. What is the current organizational structure (e.g., centralized/decentralized/functional/cross-functional/matrixed)?
2. What mix of structure will optimize innovation and empowerment?
3. How adaptive and flexible is the organization to environmental demands and opportunities?
4. How many management layers exist within the current structure?
5. What is the span of control for each management layer?
6. Have teams been formed to be responsible for a complete product or service?

Systems

1. Are organizational hardware and software aligned to achieve competitive advantage?
2. What reward and recognition systems exist for individuals and/or teams?
3. Do reward and recognition systems support the business strategy?

Skills
1. What is the maturity (skills, motivation) of the group impacted by restructuring/change?
2. Is training aligned to business needs?
3. Does the organization provide lateral and vertical expansion of skills and contributions?
4. Is the organization committed to mastery of multiple skills?
5. Is there a skills and interest inventory of current employees?

Management Style
1. Is leadership within the current structure exemplified by a top-down hierarchy of decisions and information flow or is leadership shared?
2. Do we have management styles which could disable a participative and empowering process?
3. Which stakeholders are least represented in the current state and how would the system change if their voices had equal influence?
4. Is employee input elicited and responded to?

Shared Values
1. Does the business, organization, and/or team inspire a well articulated and widely understood set of values and beliefs?
2. Does the organization have a constructive culture (emphasis on personal values, creativity, innovation) or a passive culture?

Sample Cover Letter

To: Distribution List   Date:
From: Empowerment Champion
Re: Current State Assessment

In recent weeks, Corporate has communicated several critical success factors (goals) that will position the corporation for achieving its vision of Total Customer Satisfaction. One of these critical success factors is "empowerment in a participative workplace." Recognizing that a team-based culture continues to pay dividends as an integral part of performance improvement and competitive advantage, Corporate considers a strategy of progressing to the high end of an employee-involvement continuum to be a breakthrough opportunity.

The commitment of senior management to the empowerment initiative is best demonstrated by the staffing of positions chartered with championing that change strategy within each of the sectors. My role as an internal consultant/facilitator is first to enlist your help in assessing the impact of current systems, policies/procedures, and traditions on business performance and a higher level of employee involvement. This current state assessment will yield a composite organizational view of the degree of alignment and change necessary to incorporate into actions to facilitate moving forward with the empowerment initiative.

Attached are several key questions; your responses are pertinent to providing a representation of the perceived current state. As the distribution list indicates, this questionnaire is being forwarded to a well-defined cross section of the organization to ensure a more meaningful summary. Please be honest with your responses and elaborate where necessary to better convey your thoughts or message. To encourage your response to this questionnaire, you are not required to include your name on the return, all returns will be held in confidence, names will not be identified with responses on the summary report, and you will receive a copy of the summary report.

Please return your completed questionnaire by e-mail, interoffice mail, or fax no later than one week from the date of this memo. A summarized report of responses to this questionnaire will be mailed (e-mail and hard copy) to sector senior management (as sponsors) and to the distribution list of this mailing. A subsequent memo detailing next-step actions for the empowerment initiative will follow upon completion of this summary.

If you have any questions or need any clarification, please don't hesitate to call (1-800-EMPOWER). Thank you for your time and help in this important task.

Regards,
Russell D. Robinson

Sample Distribution

To: Distribution list (random selection)

<u>Business Team (3):</u>
Product Planner X
Product Planner X
Product Manager X

<u>Compensation (3):</u>
Compensation Analyst X
Compensation Analyst X
Compensation Manager X

<u>Development Engineering (9):</u>
Hardware Engineer X
Hardware Engineer X
Software Engineer X
Software Engineer X
Software Engineer X
Mechanical Engineer X
Mechanical Engineer X
Lead Engineer X
Engineering Manager X
<u>Employee Relations (3):</u>
Employee Relations Rep X
Employee Relations Rep X
Mgr. Employee Relations X

<u>Finance (3):</u>
Cost Accountant X
Manufacturing Accountant X
Finance Manager X
<u>Information Systems (3):</u>
Programmer X
Programmer X
Information Systems Mgr. X

cc: Sr. Manager X
Sr. Manager X

<u>Manufacturing (6):</u>
Operator X
Operator X
Technician X
Team Leader X
Prod. Supervisor X
Mfg. Manager X

<u>Materials (8):</u>
Buyer X
Buyer X
Planner X
Planner X
Receiving Clerk X
Shipping Clerk X
Scheduler X
Purchasing Manager X

<u>Network Support (1):</u>
LAN Administrator X
<u>Quality Control (1):</u>
QC Engineer X

<u>Sales (4):</u>
Field Sales Rep X
Key Account Rep X
Account Executive X
Director Sales X
<u>Training (3):</u>
Training Coordinator X
Training Coordinator X
Training Manager X

DESIGN TEAM FORMATION

Just the right accompaniment for your favorite change strategy. Choose from a variety of core and/or cross-functional members. For a spicier blend, add representation from human resources, compensation, and the union(s) if applicable.

Ingredients
    1 CEO (<u>C</u>hampion of <u>E</u>mpowered <u>O</u>rganizations)
    Selected core team members
    Selected cross-functional members
    Selected support team members

Makes one serving (for manufacturing or nonmanufacturing)

1. Work with senior managers to select or solicit volunteer teams to engage in the empowerment process.
2. Solicit from team managers any cross-functional or support staff involvement needed to ensure a successful transition; secure approval from their management for active participation.
3. Conduct an empowerment workshop for team(s) to define change drivers, empowerment context, benefits, and outcomes of process.
4. Enlist volunteers from team(s) to form design team(s); set up weekly meetings.
5. Prepare document that defines team charter, implementation process, and evaluation criteria. Cover; simmer until group consensus is reached.
6. Prepare environmental scan that analyzes who in the external/internal business environment expects what from the empowered team, now and in the foreseeable future.
7. Meanwhile, gauge current and expected level of sponsorship of stakeholders. Carve out actions to be taken, where appropriate, to close expectation gaps.
8. Gradually develop a detailed implementation plan of everything it takes to get teams started and progressing along the empowerment continuum.

Variation
Substitute existing environmental scan if completed previously by senior management.

Tip
For best results and heartier flavor, design team size should be no greater than 10–12 members. Also, involve union(s) early! It is important to note that once volunteer and/or selected teams have committed to going through the empowerment process, don't let much time elapse before getting started; you don't want to lose the momentum. Typically, design team activities in this recipe take from six to eight weeks. Don't delay!

Sample Design Team Implementation Plan

Action Items	Resp.	Completion Date	Status
1. Work with sr. management to volunteer/select team(s) to champion/facilitate through the empowerment process.	Empowerment champion	8/12	Complete; three teams volunteered to pilot.
2. Discuss with volunteer/selected team managers, the impact of change drivers, empowered teams as a solution, the empowerment process model, benefits, and outcomes; solicit candidates for cross-functional and support staff involvement.	Empowerment champion	8/16	Complete; mgrs. supportive
3. Talk to identified cross-functional/support staff management for approval of their involvement.	Empowerment champion	8/18	Complete; Approved
4. Deliver empowerment training/workshop to volunteer/selected team(s), cross-functional members, and support team members.	Empowerment champion	8/22 8/23	Complete Complete
5. Delineate at training/workshop, the concept and responsibilities of the design team(s); solicit volunteers from team(s) to form design team(s). Set up weekly meetings.	Empowerment champion	8/23	Complete
6. Provide design team with selected readings on empowerment application.	Empowerment champion	8/25	Complete
7. Define charter, implementation process, and evaluation criteria for design team(s).	Design team	8/30	Complete

Sample Design Team Implementation Plan (continued)

Action Items	Resp.	Completion Date	Status
8. Complete external environmental scans; talk to external stakeholders (if appropriate) for input to complete.	Design team	9/13	
9. Complete internal environmental scans; talk to internal stakeholders (if appropriate) for input to complete.	Design team	9/27	
10. Complete sponsorship matrices.	Design team	10/4	
11. Complete as-is process maps representing each team's conversion process.	Design team	10/11	
12. Identify disconnects at each process step.	Design team	10/18	
13. Brainstorm and reach consensus on each team's vision.	Design team	10/25	
14. Select potential internal/external benchmarking opportunities; schedule.	Design team	11/1	

Design Team Formation

Sample Design Team

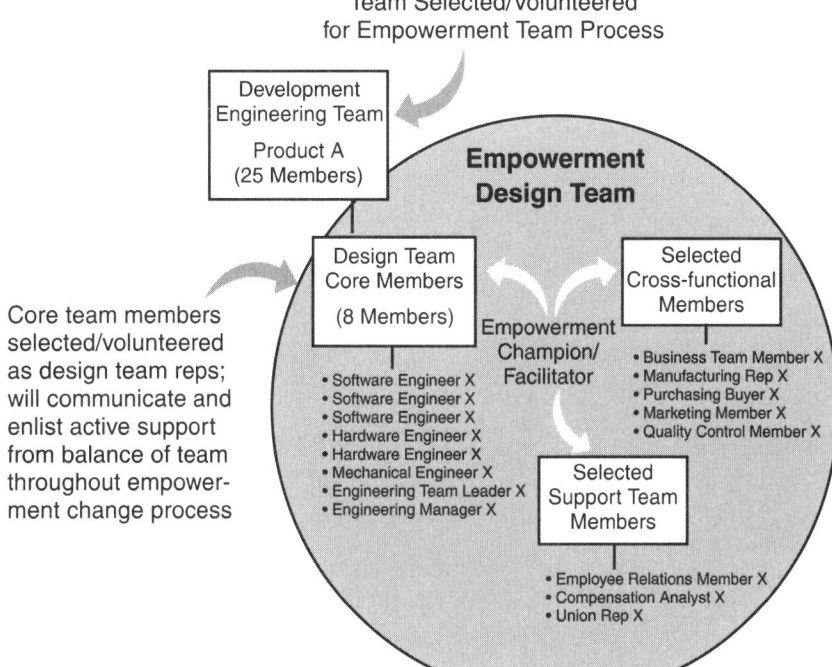

Sample Environmental Scan
Sales Team

External

Key Stake-holders	Stakeholder Needs	Stakeholder Needs That Are Not Being Met	Empowered Team Needs	Empowered Team Needs That Are Not Being Met
Customers	• Superior quality • Competitive pricing • Responsiveness • Commitment • World class support • Open architecture • Respect for culture • Flexible systems • Pre and postsale support • Product enhancement value	✓	• Clarification of needs • Sharing of information • Honest feedback • Customer's vision • Proper representation • Access to decision makers • Negotiate in good faith	✓ ✓ ✓
Regulatory bodies	• Compliance • Spectral efficient • Technology training • Economic development	 ✓	• Well defined documents • Timeliness on processes • Access to policy makers • Evaluate with open mind	 ✓
Suppliers	• Sharing of information • Timely requirements • Accurate requirements • Commitment • Partnership	✓	• Responsiveness • Fair pricing • Commitment	

Sample Environmental Scan (concluded)

Internal

Key Stakeholders	Stakeholder Needs	Stakeholder Needs That Are Not Being Met	Empowered Team Needs	Empowered Team Needs That Are Not Being Met
Management	• Satisfied customers		• Global vision	✓
	• Manage customer expectations	✓	• Customer support	
	• Manage customer relationships		• Participation	
	• Exceed job requirements		• Commitment to customers	
	• Profitable business		• Communication	✓
	• *Empowerment*	✓	• Recognition	✓
	• Meet budgets	✓		
	• Continuous improvement			
Strategic marketing	• Requirements definition		• Knowledge of requirements	
	• Prioritization		• Act as a resource	
	• Sharing competitive data		• Share information/models	
	• Strategy collaboration	✓	• Strategy collaboration	✓
Finance	• Achieve business goals		• Fair budget allocation	✓
	• Profitable business		• Communication	
	• Due diligence		• Collaboration in forecasting	
	• Acquire/verify customer's business plan	✓	• Collaboration in planning	✓
			• Collaboration in budgeting	
Mfg.	• Accurate information		• Accurate information	✓
	• Sharing of information		• Sharing of information	
	• Responsiveness	✓	• Responsiveness	
			• Increased productivity	

Sample Sponsorship Matrix

Stakeholder	Make	Help	Let	Against	Comments
VP marketing		O	X		
VP operations	O	X			
Engineering mgr.		O	X		
Team leaders	O		X		
Facilities crew			O	X	

Stakeholder	What	Who	Due Date	Status
VP marketing	Hold meetings	Champion	3/11	Complete
VP operations	Involve in planning	Champion and/or design team	3/4	Complete
Engineering mgr.	Hold meetings	Champion	3/12	Rescheduled
Team leaders	Empowerment training	Facilitator	3/6	Complete
Facilities crew	Meetings	Design team	3/16	Scheduled

Developing a Sponsorship Matrix

1. List the stakeholders who must sponsor the design and change strategy.
2. Identify their current level of sponsorship by placing an X in the appropriate column.
3. Determine the level of sponsorship needed from them, and place an O
4. For those stakeholders who need to move to new sponsorship levels, transfer their names to the lower matrix.
5. Identify what actions can be taken to shift their commitment.
6. Identify who will be responsible, the due date, and the first status check.

Source: Adapted from *Developing Self-Managing Teams,* © Abe Raab and Wilts Alexander, ASAPublishing, 1991. Reprinted with permission.

AS-IS PROCESS MAP

For added flair, serve an assortment of triangles, squares, circles, and/or rectangles mixed with arrows. Garnish with text.

Ingredients:
- Inputs
- Process steps
- Activities
- Outputs
- Disconnects

Makes one serving (for manufacturing or nonmanufacturing)

1. Arrange current process steps, representing the organization's or team's conversion process, into a sequential flow diagram. (An as-is process map draws a sequence of what steps the process actually follows at that time.)
2. Add specific inputs to and outputs from (inputs to next process step) until diagram serves as an accurate representation of the conversion process.
3. For each process step, garnish text with a list of the major activities that will convert inputs into outputs. Let stand.
4. For added flavor, identify the individual(s) responsible for performing the major activities of each process step.
5. Meanwhile, identify realized or potential disconnects (key issues arising from the way the process or participant responsibility is currently defined) that occur at each process step. List. (Disconnects, by definition, are steps, inputs or outputs, or measurements in the process that are missing, non-value-added, or performing poorly.)
6. Serve.

Variation
Process map can be developed by facilitating input via group setting or by collecting process step segments from those responsible, then assembling diagram.

Tip

For best results, prepare the process map with input from current process step participants. Also, when identifying disconnects, since it is common to document large numbers of disconnects, focus on the critical ones; you will deal with those more effectively!

Sample As-Is Process Map

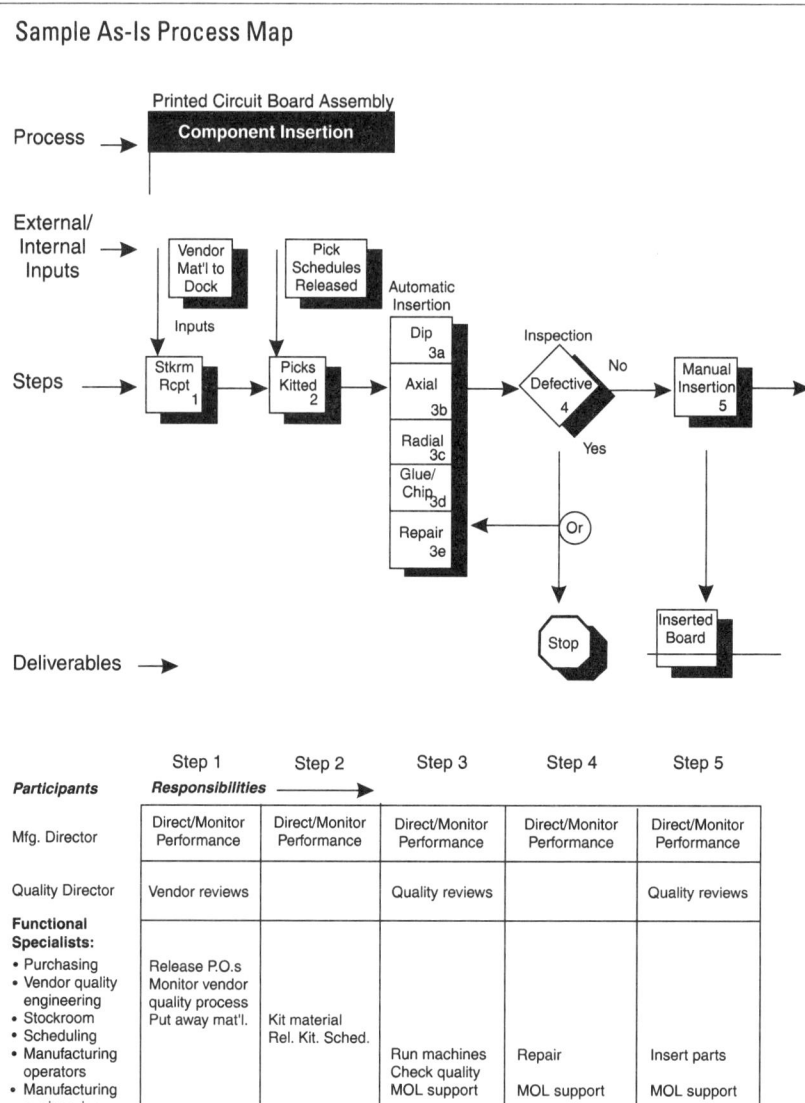

Sample Process Map Disconnects

Disconnects or Gap Analysis
Process: Insertion—Printed Circuit Board Assembly

Process Step	Process-Driven Issues	Accountability-Driven Issues
1	Parts improperly marked Vendor overruns received	Lost material Lost paperwork
2		Lack of checks & balances
3	Lack of SPC tools Machine programs inaccurate	Maintenance program slippage Lack of operator training
4	Ineffective inspection tools Analyzing queue	Lack of training
5	Improper lighting Poor fixturing	Insufficient defect tracking

FUTURE STATE VISION

Create an authentic and enticing vision, adding inputs from various organizational levels and/or team members of a shared destination over a future specified time frame.

Ingredients
   Critical unique strategic advantage(s)
   Beliefs and values
   Group interaction

Makes multiple servings (for manufacturing or nonmanufacturing

1. In a conference room or setting of appropriate size, facilitate a brainstorming session to identify the team's or organization's preferred ideal future state.
2. Identify the unique critical strategic advantage(s) that distinguishes the organization and/or team in the minds of their customers.
3. Fold in the personal values and beliefs upon which the vision is founded.
4. Stir mixture until focusing and empowering statements convey a picture of a shared destination.
5. Test vision with sponsors and other organization members to gain insight into vision's possible acceptance and/or refinement. Mix until smooth.
6. Serve. Let stand.

Variation
A vision can be prepared by facilitating a brainstorming session with the team or by receiving and blending individual member input, followed by the task of reaching consensus.

Tip
Many organizations are unaware of the power that a vision produces. Vision is a catalyst for change. Vision is creating a preferred future, a shared destination of what you want the team or organization to be. Your challenge is to make sure that each and every team member is involved in creating the vision; this will inspire commitment and create ownership.

The creation of an agreed-upon vision rarely happens in a single session—be patient! A vision should be articulated in one or more short, simple statements. For crispness and authenticity, allot the appropriate amount of time to craft a vision. Remember, how the words get written is just as important as what gets written!

Sample Future State Vision

Empowerment Process Model
Planning Elements

Manufacturing Recipes:

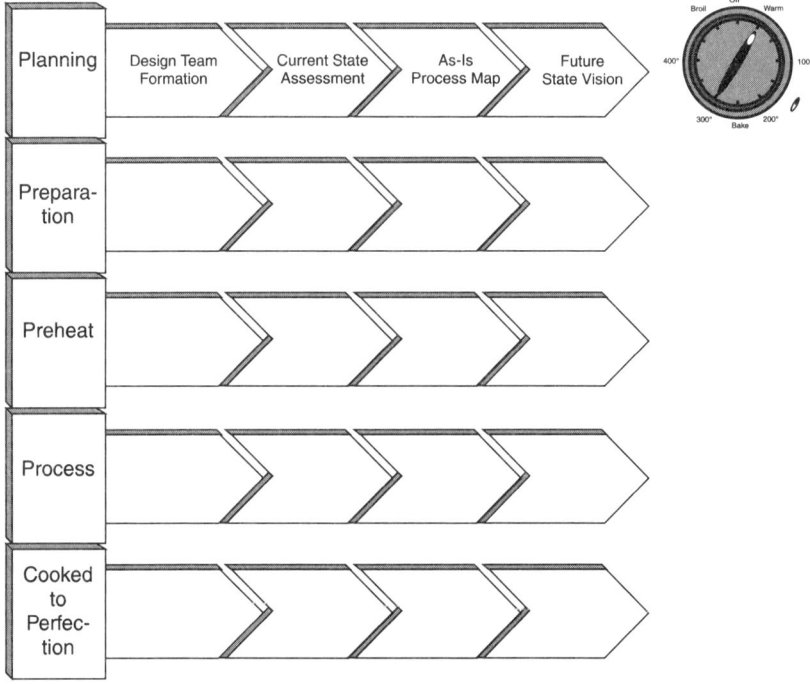

Empowerment Process Model
Planning Elements

Nonmanufacturing Recipes:

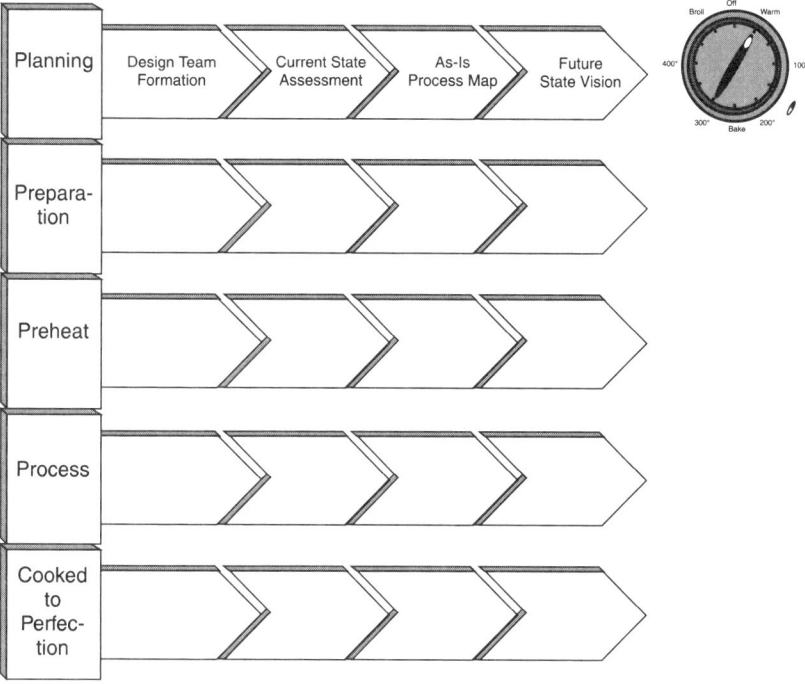

SUMMARY

Empowerment is a process and not a destination. As you move through the planning stage, some will find it difficult to admit that the current state is less than perfect, and even more challenging to accept it. As a Champion of Empowered Organizations, you will be tested time and time again, relative to the need for change, its merit, and the effort it will take to get there. Show the slightest waning of your dedication to the empowerment vision, and chance a diminishing level of support. Model the behavior and be firm in your conviction!

The planning element is critical in that it sets the stage for realizing that the way things are today will not suffice for success tomorrow. Recipes in this planning collection have more than likely reinforced or provided realization of a dissatisfaction with the current state and crafted a vision for a new tomorrow.

Know that at this stage of the process model, you have become visible to the management hierarchy and the depths of the organization. No matter what the organization's history relative to embracing change has been, remember that you are just one more proponent. The task ahead will certainly test the effectiveness of your skills as a facilitator and mentor, as well as your patience.

The appetizer for a change strategy has been served, and the temperature of the organization is getting warm!

PART TWO

PREPARATION

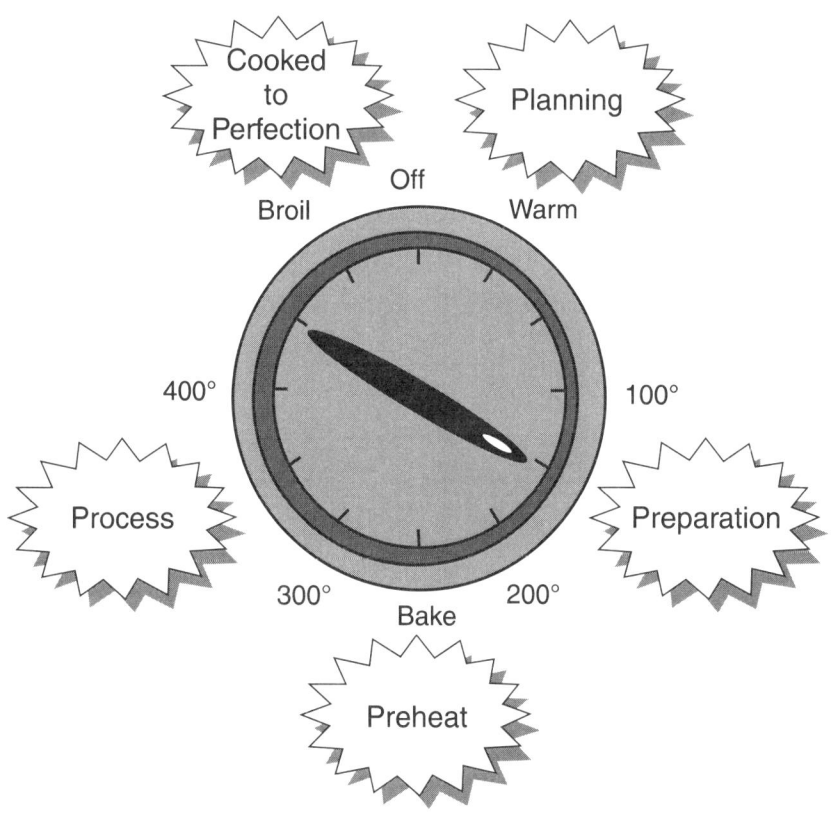

PREPARATION

The "Preparation" part of this book is brimming with recipes guaranteed to serve a successful launch of empowered teams. New and experienced champions alike will savor these versatile dishes representing some traditional favorites!

Preparation begins with formulating a mission statement that conveys the specific purpose of the team within the time frame of the future vision. *Specific* is a key word here, as a broad-based mission will make it difficult for a team to feel ownership and impact performance. Take the time necessary to develop the context of the mission, as it will reinforce performance expectations and behaviors.

The next step in the empowerment preparation process is identifying the specific areas of focus that will serve to measure progress against the mission. Within this element of the process model begins a divergence of recipes for manufacturing and nonmanufacturing.

The objectives matrix performs as a yardstick for measuring manufacturing team effort and mixes well as an effective element in team-based pay concepts. Blend in management input and be sure to align with the overall business strategy!

Completing a skills inventory for the manufacturing organization or team follows the development of the objective matrix. Assessing basic skills (basic education) and technical skill capability will provide a foundation from which to evaluate the ability of the organization or team to maximize performance and to develop and implement required training.

Goal preparation for nonmanufacturing organizations or teams may not be as easy as it is for manufacturing. Many of the objectives for the latter are classic standards, while the former presents a case for a wide variation based on function or structure. Essential to measuring progress against team purpose, nonmanufacturing goals must also be linked to the overall business strategy!

Finally, creating a should-be process map representing the organization's or team's ideal future conversion process completes this phase. The outcome of the change process has been documented and provides incentive for the challenges ahead.

You are now ready to select the preparation recipes that will continue the empowerment journey. Sample the featured entrees as desired. Prepare well—the change process is underway!

MISSION

Here's a spin-off of the popular future state vision entree and sure to be a hit with team members. Serve as statement(s) identifying the specific purpose of the team or organization.

Ingredients
    1 future state vision
    Group interaction

Makes one serving (for manufacturing or nonmanufacturing)

1. In a conference room or setting of appropriate size, facilitate a brainstorming session to identify the team's or organization's specific purpose of existence, for now and the foreseeable future.
2. Blend inputs, stirring often.
3. Test mission with sponsors and other organization members to gain insight into mission's acceptance and/or refinement. Add to mixture.
4. Firmly shape into a condensed statement of purpose. Let stand.

Variation
Prepare the sponsorship input in advance to blend in during brainstorming.

Tip
A mission statement helps team members to connect and identify with what the team is. It is a statement of what the business is or is expected to be over a future time frame. It is the team's purpose and reason for existence. It is important to establish the difference between a vision and a mission statement. Remember, a vision is a shared destination of what you want the team or organization to be. A mission statement articulates how a team will achieve its vision. The objective of a mission statement is to promote dialogue about who the team is, what the team does, and its purpose.

    Like preparing a vision, a purposeful and effective mission statement probably will not be created in a single session; patience is a virtue! Finally, know that preparing a concise and specific mission statement(s) will save valuable goal-setting time.

Sample Mission

International Sales Team Mission
Establish Product A as a profitable international wireless business by focusing on today's opportunities with today's solutions, while frequently assessing future regional customer needs and product requirements, and developing strategies for continuously increasing regional market share percentages during Product A's life cycle.

Development Engineering Team Mission
Product B's team will contribute to company profitability by developing infrastructure products and services that meet and exceed customer needs, are delivered to regional markets in opportunistic time-to-market speed, and minimize resource investment and costs.

Manufacturing Team Mission
Establish manufacturing leadership of Product C radio system solutions through quality, delivery speed, and cost performance. Maximize performance capability by utilizing state-of-the-art technology and flexible, highly skilled, empowered work teams.

OBJECTIVES MATRIX

One of manufacturing's most requested recipes! Serve with classic measures or add others as desired.

Ingredients
    1 mission statement(s)
    Group interaction
    Corporate, sector, or site continuous improvement targets

Makes multiple servings (for manufacturing)

1. In a conference room or setting of appropriate size, facilitate a brainstorming session to identify the specific areas of focus that will gauge progress against the mission statement.
2. Meanwhile, whip up a separate list identifying specific management required objectives. Add.
3. Blend inputs. Carve out objectives that are aligned to the overall business strategy. Simmer until consensus is reached.
4. Determine the definition and formula for each objective.
5. Garnish with performance goals from agreed-upon baseline and incorporate annual corporate-, sector-, site-, or team-derived percentage improvement targets.
6. Spread weighting factors across objectives, totalling 100 percent.
7. Assign point value scheme to measure team(s) on a weekly, quarterly, and annual basis.
8. Test objectives with sponsors and other organization members to gain insight into acceptance and/or refinement.
9. Serve. For added flavor, post result updates in visible areas for team accessibility and monitor.

Variation
Substitute any objectives pertinent to business performance.

Tip
For zest, increase the baseline each year to help drive continuous improvement! To gain acceptance or sustain momentum, influence or suggest changes to the compensation system to incorporate a team-based pay concept.

Sample Objectives Matrix

Objectives Matrix Data

Year:

Objective	Unit of Measure	Definition/Formula	Annual Improvement Target*
Quality	PPB (parts per billion)	Escaping defects and internal defects (test found) divided by total opportunities multiplied by 1,000,000	68%
Service level	% (percent)	Weighted kanban and schedule	50%
Cost	$ Cost per unit	Direct labor dollars per component placed	20%
Cycle time	Hour	Average cycle time from start process to end process	50%
Employee Suggestions	Average suggestions per member	Employee suggestions submitted divided by factory headcount	20
Training	% (percent)	Members with 40 hours training divided by total members	100%
Factory audits	% (percent)	Compliance with factory audits	100%
Scrap	% (percent)	Scrap dollars per material dollars fabbed	30%

* Annual corporate-, sector-, site-, or team-derived improvement targets, except "employee suggestions."

Team Performance Evaluation and Scoring

Team performance: Evaluate the extent to which team's performance meets established objectives.

Score	
4.0	The team consistently exceeds established objectives
3.0	The team consistently meets and sometimes exceeds established objectives
2.0	The team consistently meets established objectives
1.0	The team achieves sporadic results and only sometimes meets established objectives
0	The team very rarely meets any established objectives

Team performance scoring resembles that of individual and/or peer performance evaluation for use in a team-based pay compensation system.

Annual Corporate-, Sector-, Site-, or Team-Derived Percentage Improvement Targets, with Team Performance Evaluation Scoring

Point Value	Quality	Service Level*	Cost	Cycle Time	Employee Suggestions	Training	Audits	Scrap**
4.0	68%	50%	20%	50%	20	100.0%	100%	30%
3.5	51%	37%	15%	37%	18	97.5%	95%	25%
3.0	34%	25%	10%	25%	16	95.0%	90%	20%
2.5	17%	12%	5%	12%	14	92.5%	85%	15%
2.0	0%	0%	0%	0%	12	90.0%	80%	10%
1.5	−15%	−12%	−5%	−5%	10	87.5%	75%	5%
1.0	−30%	−25%	−10%	−10%	8	85.0%	70%	0%
0	<−30%	<−25%	<−10%	<−10%	<8	<85.0%	<70%	<0%
Weight	25%	25%	20%	10%	5%	5%	5%	5%

* Service level objective can be replaced with productivity in nonservice areas.
** Scrap objective can be replaced with inventory integrity in material stores locations.

In most cases, the baseline is derived by annualizing the team's averaged performance over the previous two quarters. In this example and those that follow, a point value of 2.0 was considered to represent average performance, and the baseline was set as such. A weighting factor is assigned to each objective by the team based on their perception of that objective's relative importance to the overall business strategy. The sum of weighting factors is equal to 100 percent.

Objectives Matrix
Improvement Model: Quality

Point Value	Wk 1	Wk 2	Wk 3	Wk 4	Wk 5	Wk 26	Wk 40	Wk 52
4.0	1.3%	2.6%	3.9%	5.2%	6.5%	34.0%	52.0%	68.0%
3.5	1.0%	1.9%	2.9%	3.9%	4.9%	25.0%	39.0%	51.0%
3.0	0.7%	1.3%	1.9%	2.6%	3.3%	17.0%	26.0%	34.0%
2.5	0.3%	0.7%	1.0%	1.3%	1.6%	8.5%	13.0%	17.0%
2.0	0.0%	0.0%	0.0%	0.0%	0.0%	0.0%	0.0%	0.0%
1.5	−0.3%	−0.6%	−0.9%	−1.2%	−1.4%	−7.5%	−11.5%	−15.0%
1.0	−0.6%	−1.2%	−1.7%	−2.3%	−2.9%	−15.0%	−23.0%	−30.0%
0	<−0.6%	<−1.2%	<−1.7%	<−2.3%	<−2.9%	<−15.0%	<−23.0%	<−30.0%

Based on either corporate-, sector-, site-, or team-derived annual percentage improvement targets, weekly targets are calculated and point values assigned for each objective.

Objectives Matrix
Team Performance Quarterly Summary

Wk	Quality	Service Level	Cost	Cycle Time	Employee Suggestions	Training	Audits	Scrap	Team Perf.
1	0	4	4	0	1	0	3.5	4	2.2
2	0	4	0	0	4	0	2.5	4	1.5
3	4	4	4	0	4	0	1.5	4	3.3
4	0	0	4	0	4	0	3.5	0	1.2
5	0	3.5	4	0	1	0	3.5	0	1.9
6	4	4	4	0	1	0	3.5	4	3.2
7	1.5	4	4	0	1	0	2.5	4	2.6
8	4	4	4	4	0	0	3	4	3.6
9	0	4	4	0	0	0	2	0	1.9
10	0	4	4	4	0	0	2	4	2.5
11	3.5	4	4	4	0	0	2	4	3.4
12	0	4	0	4	4	0	3.5	4	2.0
13	0	4	0	0	4	0	3	4	1.6
Q1	1.3	3.7	3.1	1.2	1.8	0.0	2.8	3.1	2.4
Wt	25%	25%	20%	10%	5%	5%	5%	5%	

The Objectives Matrix measures teams on a weekly basis for each objective. Teams can earn from 0 to 4.0 points, measured in half-point increments. Again, a weekly point total is calculated by comparing actual performance to the annual improvement target divided by 52 weeks. A weekly team performance is calculated by multiplying each objective times its corresponding weighting factor and then averaging scores for the eight objectives.

Objectives Matrix
Team Performance Summary (Year)

Wk	Quality	Service Level	Cost	Cycle Time	Employee Suggestions	Training	Audits	Scrap	Team Perf.
Q1	1.3	3.7	3.1	1.2	1.8	0.0	2.8	3.1	2.4
Q2	2.0	3.5	2.0	2.5	2.0	2.0	3.5	4.0	2.6
Q3	3.5	3.0	1.8	2.3	2.5	3.0	4.0	3.6	2.9
Q4	1.0	3.7	3.1	1.2	1.8	0.0	2.8	3.1	2.4
Yr.	2.0	3.5	2.5	1.8	2.0	1.3	3.3	3.5	2.5
Wt.	25%	25%	20%	10%	5%	5%	5%	5%	

Weekly scores are averaged to produce a single score each quarter. Team performance for the year is derived by averaging the four quarters.

SKILLS INVENTORY

A great make-ahead recipe, complete with a skills profile for each employee. Serve topped with a training plan.

Ingredients
>1 vision
>1 mission statement(s)
>1 as-is process map
>1 design team
>Selected cross-functional members (i.e., human resources, training, and union(s), if applicable)

Makes one serving (for manufacturing)

1. Prepare a rough draft skills assessment strategy proposal. Reference vision/mission and frame anticipated skills required in future state. Mix.
2. Test strategy proposal with management, sponsors and union(s), if applicable, for acceptance and/or refinement.
3. Seek legal counsel relative to skills assessment strategy boundaries, assessment instruments, application, and communication. Shape aggregate direct labor manufacturing employee assessment strategy.
4. Communicate skills assessment strategy intent, impact, and timing to manufacturing. Position as strategic link to vision/mission, job enrichment, and personal growth for employees.
5. Conduct job analysis to determine distinguishing competencies for each task in as-is process. Techniques vary; select one or combine to capture appropriate data. Options include:
   - ✔ Structured interviews.
   - ✔ Observation.
   - ✔ Checklists.
   - ✔ Focus groups.
   - ✔ Daily, weekly, monthly logs.
   - ✔ Commercial products.

6. Validate job analysis with independent (2nd) group of subject matter experts to ensure quality of information collected.
7. Establish skill baseline for each task, process, or targeted factory operation using either internal assessment instruments, appropriate commercial products with best-fit application, or external consultant. Let stand.
8. Manage the change process. Examples include:
   ✔ Develop training curriculum; implement.
   ✔ Redesign job(s).
   ✔ Match person to position.
9. Evaluate program effectiveness relative to enhanced skills transfer to task/job and impact to individual, organization, and business.

Variation
Use external expertise in conducting job analysis, determining skill baselines, and administering training if resources and/or experience are unavailable.

Tip
Prepare list of anticipated questions arising from formal communication of skills assessment strategy. Formulate best answers to questions as a guide for those communicating strategy or those in leadership roles who may be asked questions during or after communication.

Sample Skills Inventory

Current State:

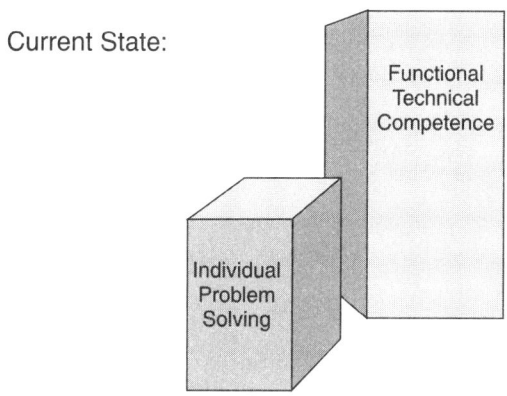

Future State
Skills Assessment:

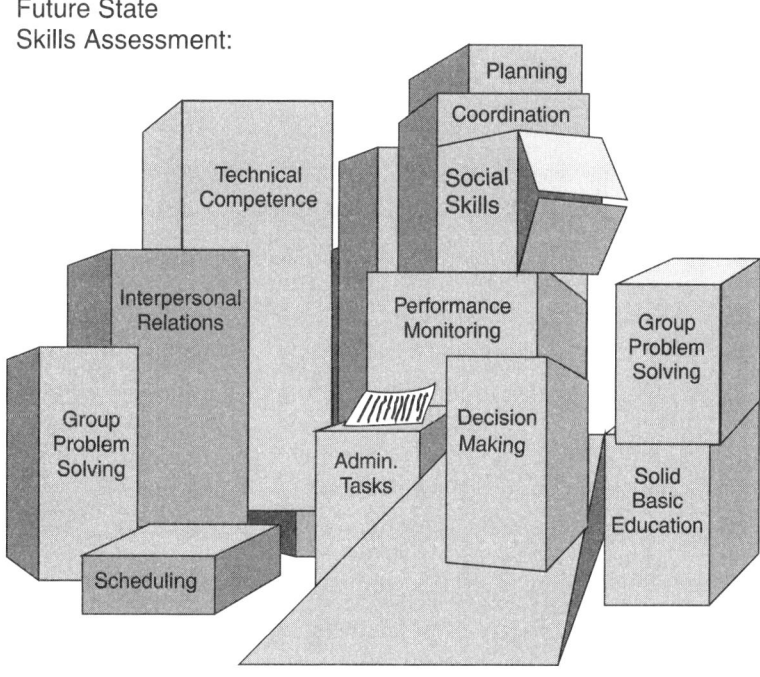

GOALS

More popular than ever, this entree has been a classic with management, but our taste testers throughout the organization delight in this serving.

Ingredients
>1 mission statement(s)
>Roadmaps (product, technology, process, tools, etc.), if applicable
>Long range plan (financial), if applicable
>Group interaction

Makes multiple servings (for nonmanufacturing)

1. In a conference room or setting of appropriate size, facilitate a brainstorming session to identify the specific areas of focus that will gauge progress against a team's mission. (Goal statements are task oriented and describe specific accomplishments or milestones that will need to be achieved if a team is to make progress on their mission. Goals may be short-term or long-term but should always represent distinct, measurable challenges that require a team's collective focus, actions, and attention.)

2. Blend inputs. Carve out goals that are aligned to the overall business strategy. Simmer until consensus is reached. (Understanding the organization's business strategy is critical when establishing team goals. Several inputs that can be valuable to a team in grasping the overall business strategy are roadmaps and long range plans. Roadmaps—product, technology, process, tools, and so on—are documented current and future business plans that depict the strategic evolution of the product, process, or service direction that a business intends to take. Roadmaps typically define the business direction for the next 5 to 10 years. Securing long-range plan data (financial) can provide a team with relevant information as to the anticipated growth rate—sales, revenue, market share—of the business.)

3. Prepare goal definitions and formulas. (For each goal that a team selects, write a statement of intended accomplishment and the methodology and/or formula that will be the measure for tracking performance vs. goal.)
4. Garnish with performance goals from agreed upon baseline and incorporate annual corporate-, sector-, site-, or team-derived percentage improvement targets. (It has been my experience that higher levels of management, such as corporate, sector, and the like, will define annual performance improvement targets for many key initiatives, like quality and cycle time, that teams will be expected to comply with.)
5. Test goals with sponsors and other organization members to gain insight into acceptance and/or refinement.
6. Cool and serve.

Variation
Substitute team developed roadmaps and/or long-range plans if that data is not already available.

Tip
At this stage of the empowerment process, it may be difficult for teams to secure strategic information (e.g., roadmaps, long-range plans). First, management may be reluctant to share information considered to be strategic and/or proprietary with a wider audience. It may be necessary for teams or the champion(s) to justify requesting such information. Secondly, strategic information may not exist or be available in a form that can be understood or used by teams. Finally, if roadmaps and long-range plans are currently developed beyond team scope and structure, look for opportunities to have teams participate in the development of that information.

Sample Goals

International Sales Team Goals
1. Achieve current-year release plan of $125M.
   Milestones
   ✔ Q1 release of $25M.
   ✔ Q2 release of $25M; YTD cumulative release of $50M.
   ✔ Q3 release of $35M; YTD cumulative release of $85M.
   ✔ Q4 release of $40M; YTD cumulative release of $125M.
2. Achieve current-year ship plan of $100M.
   Milestones
   ✔ Q1 ship of $20M
   ✔ Q2 ship of $20M; YTD cumulative ship of $40M
   ✔ Q3 ship of $25M; YTD cumulative ship of $65M
   ✔ Q4 ship of $35M; YTD cumulative ship of $100M
3. Establish a postsale customer support process (loading/expansion/marketing) by the end of the year.
   Milestones
   ✔ Preliminary plan by Q1, current year.
   ✔ Final draft by Q2, current year.
   ✔ Implementation by Q3, current year.

SHOULD-BE PROCESS MAP

This flavorful entree is a culinary delight. Sponsors and team members alike will want larger portions!

Ingredients
    1 As-is process map
    Inputs
    Process Steps
    Activities
    Outputs

Makes one serving (for manufacturing or nonmanufacturing)

1. Arrange process steps, representing organization's or team's ideal future conversion process, into a sequential flow diagram. (A should-be process map draws a sequence of what steps a process should follow if everything was ideal or worked correctly.)
2. Add specific inputs to and outputs from (inputs to next process step) until diagram serves as an accurate representation of the conversion process.
3. For each process step, garnish with text a list of the major activities that will convert inputs into outputs. Let stand.
4. For added flavor, identify the team members(s) responsible for performing the major activities of each process step.
5. Meanwhile, identify potential disconnects. Carve out actions to eliminate at source.
6. Serve.

Variation
Slice ideal future conversion process into sections and complete. Let stand. Repeat above steps for each section.

Tip
Review list of disconnects from as-is process map in prior planning stage to make sure they have been minimized or eliminated in should-be process map.

Sample Should-Be Process Map

As-Is Process Map

Process → Printed Circuit Board Assembly / **Component Insertion**

External/Internal Inputs → ~~Vendor Mat'l to Dock~~, ~~Pick Schedules Released~~

Steps → ~~Stkrm Pool 1~~, ~~Picks Kitted 2~~, Automatic Insertion (Dip 3a, Axial 3b, Radial 3c, Glue/Chip 3d, ~~Repair 3e~~) → Inspection Defective? → No → Manual Insertion 5; Yes → Or → Stop

Deliverables → Inserted Board

Should-Be Process Map

Process → Printed Circuit Board Assembly / **Component Insertion**

External/Internal Inputs → Vendor Mat'l to Floor

Steps → Automatic Insertion ("State of the Art" Technology): Picks Kitted 1a, Dip 1b, Axial 1c, Radial 1d, Glue/Chip 1e → Maximized migration of manually inserted parts to automatic insertion → Manual Insertion 2

Deliverables → Inserted Board

Empowerment Process Model
Preparation Elements

Manufacturing Recipes:

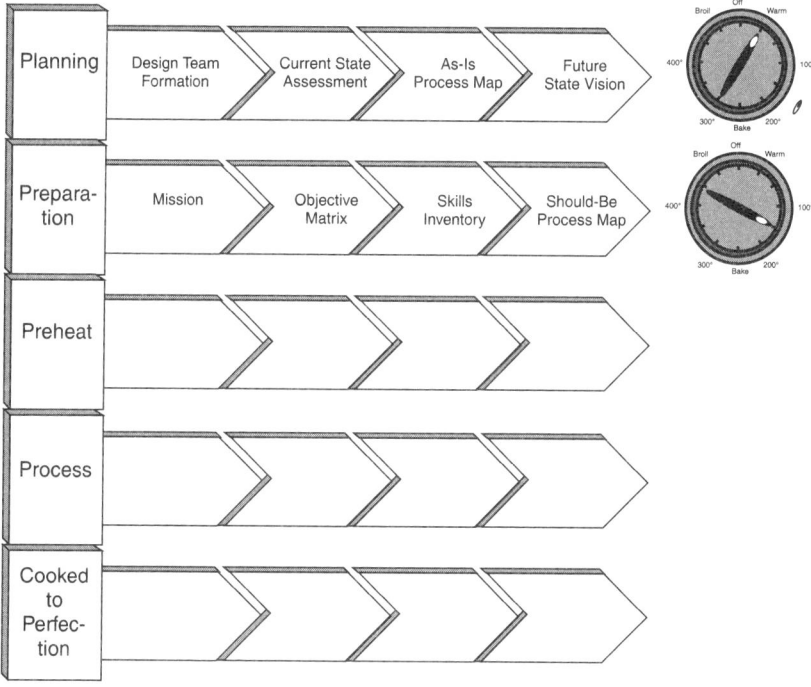

Empowerment Process Model
Preparation Elements

Nonmanufacturing Recipes:

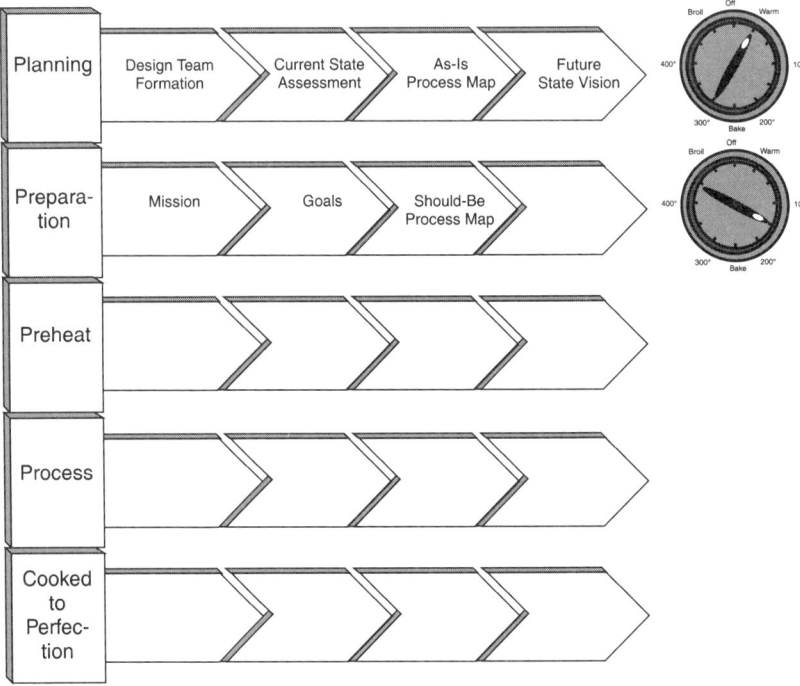

SUMMARY

Constancy of purpose is a major ingredient of success. As you begin the preparation stage, it is imperative for the team to craft a well defined and articulated statement of purpose. Shaping and crafting a mission in participation with those who will live it will enhance commitment. Participation produces empowerment and that will empower its use and effectiveness. As a Champion of Empowered Organizations, your task is to facilitate consensus for the right mission. The interactive process of reaching consensus will test your mettle, because many individuals will interpret team purpose differently. Listen, blend, shape, and build acceptance!

Having a mission statement isn't enough, however. What gets measured gets done. Identifying and measuring specific areas of focus that gauge progress against the mission is critical in creating intent and for staying on the right course.

Once goals and/or objectives are established and measurement criteria defined, don't hesitate in collecting data and tracking performance. Formulating a baseline will render the distance of the journey in either direction; the results can sometimes be humbling.

Finally, assessing the critical skill requirements in the ideal future conversion process and comparing them to the existing skills profile for each employee will help to specify the magnitude of the training effort. It will take time not only to develop and/or source, but to implement the right training. Execution to performance expectations may not happen as quickly as desired. Be patient but press on!

Preparation for the change strategy is now complete; the temperature of the organization is rising!

PART THREE

PREHEAT

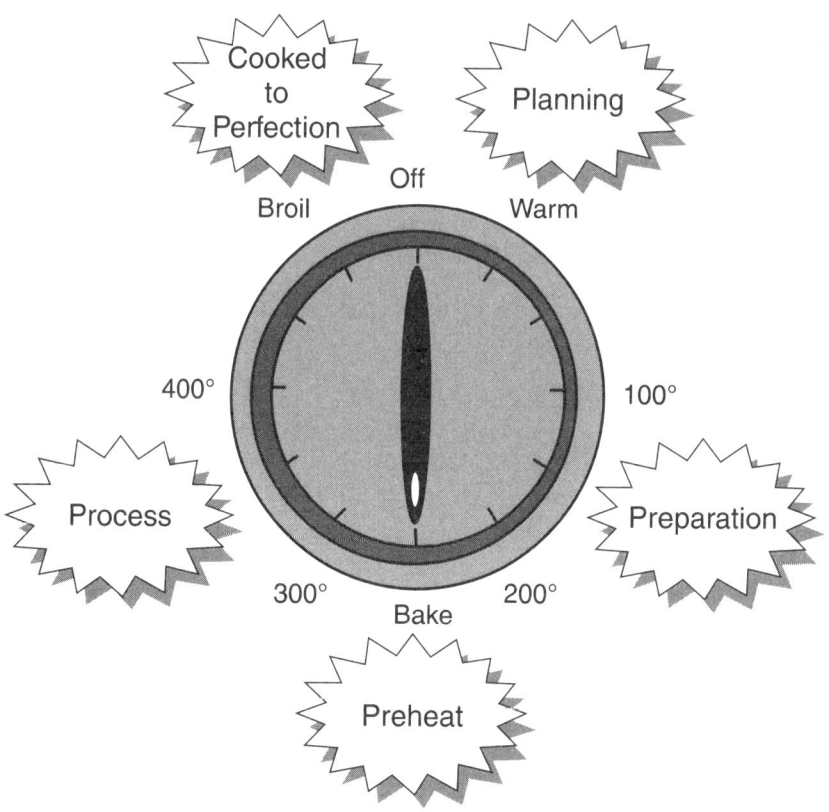

PREHEAT

Recipe collections in the "Preheat" part of this book will warm the organization to the concept of empowerment! Champions will savor the interaction and involvement as team activities heat up, while teamwork and responsiveness will add flavor to a culture on the brink of change.

Preheat begins for manufacturing with a champion organizing and facilitating flash meetings (not that kind!). Aptly named for the short duration and frequency of meetings, the concept is to evolve team dialogue relative to customer needs, team performance, and response. The purpose is to develop quick decision-making capability and ownership of performance.

Manufacturing's cross-training matrix provides a visible record of process or task mastery and doubles as a forward-looking training plan. Prepared well, this template will leave little doubt as to current and projected team capability!

Preheat begins for nonmanufacturing with the physical co-location of team members. Co-location will enhance communication, foster commitment, and provide focus on quick response. Greater awareness of the big picture and role clarity will prove invaluable as the empowerment journey continues.

The importance of functional parity cannot be overstated. Keeping everyone on the same level of importance will lend to a successful mix. Each team member's contribution is of equal value in achieving expectations for business success.

The next step in the empowerment preheat stage is benchmarking. Literature, seminars/workshops, and internal/external best-practice empowered teams provide numerous opportunities to gauge progress, answer questions, and learn from what others have experienced. Involving the team in benchmarking will reinforce the concept and vision that you as a champion have been evolving.

Finally, customer visits or at best, other voice-of-the-customer equivalent tools, will increase sensitivity to customer needs and instill a feeling of ownership and pride. The challenge is to listen and incorporate customer input into a product, process, or service that delights the customer.

You are now ready to select the preheat recipes that will continue the empowerment journey. Select these entrees as the situation requires. Better yet, bake all the way through to acquire a taste for additional servings!

FLASH MEETING

A hot combo with the objectives matrix—most take 10 minutes or less. You'll need a minimum of two servings per shift.

Ingredients

> 1 Champion of Empowered Organizations or design team member
>
> 1 egg timer
>
> Direct labor manufacturing teams (process or functional)

Makes one serving (for manufacturing)

1. Communicate concept and purpose of flash meetings to manufacturing teams. Concept is to facilitate information flow within team structure relative to customer needs (internal/external), determine and execute plans to meet customer needs, and raise other critical team issues requiring action. Purpose is to develop team decision-making capability and ownership of business performance. Simmer.
2. Select one to three critical manufacturing objectives from the objectives matrix for daily shift focus (e.g., units produced, quality, service level).
3. Slice weekly targets (as identified in objectives matrix for selected measures) into hourly targets. For multiple shifts with unbalanced head count, prorate targets based on roster head count for each shift, the sum of which is equal to the total daily target for each day of the current workweek.
4. Prepare a matrix of cumulative hourly and week targets covering all shifts for selected measures (above) for each day of current workweek, using media that team members can use for posting cumulative actual hourly and week performance (poster board, paper, computer screens, etc.). Station, post, or hang matrix in highly visible team location. (See sample flash meeting exhibit.)
5. Choose several meeting times during the course of a shift, including shift overlaps, to discuss team progress relative

to hourly and week targets for selected measures. The meeting is to last no longer than 10 minutes. Meeting is to take place at the location where the objectives matrix is stationed, posted, or hung. There should be at least two 10-minute meetings (flash meetings) per shift, with a recommendation for as many as four per shift; continue until team understands purpose.
6. Set egg timer for 10 minutes.
7. Have team post cumulative hourly and week performance actuals to selected measures since last flash meeting.
8. Engage team by questioning as to why team is behind target if cumulative actuals are less than target performance, and what action(s) the team is going to take to achieve targets by the next flash meeting or by the end of the work day/week. If cumulative actuals are greater than targets, ask the team about actions that will maintain that performance or use time for problem solving. Should meeting extend the full 10 minutes, meeting is ended when egg timer goes off, regardless of incompleteness of discussion. (Note: champion's role is to facilitate response and consensus as to actions. Encourage the team to try actions that they feel are appropriate. However, recognize discouragement and respond by coaching team to a right course of action(s). Intent of setting the egg timer for 10 minutes is to foster a quick decision-making process. Flash meetings at shift change or overlap will promote better communication and follow-up. As flash meetings evolve, the champion's role is to become less involved as a facilitator and coach, eventually transitioning responsibility to the team.)
9. Cool.

Variation
After initial servings of Flash Meetings, encourage the team to rotate team members into various roles such as: customer interface, management interface, safety champion, team leader, and the like, to understand the mix of activities required in day to day execution.

Tip
Involve cross-functional participation in flash meetings (representation from internal customers, internal suppliers, scheduling, manufacturing engineering, etc.). This will improve communication, teamwork, performance, and ownership!

Sample Flash Meeting

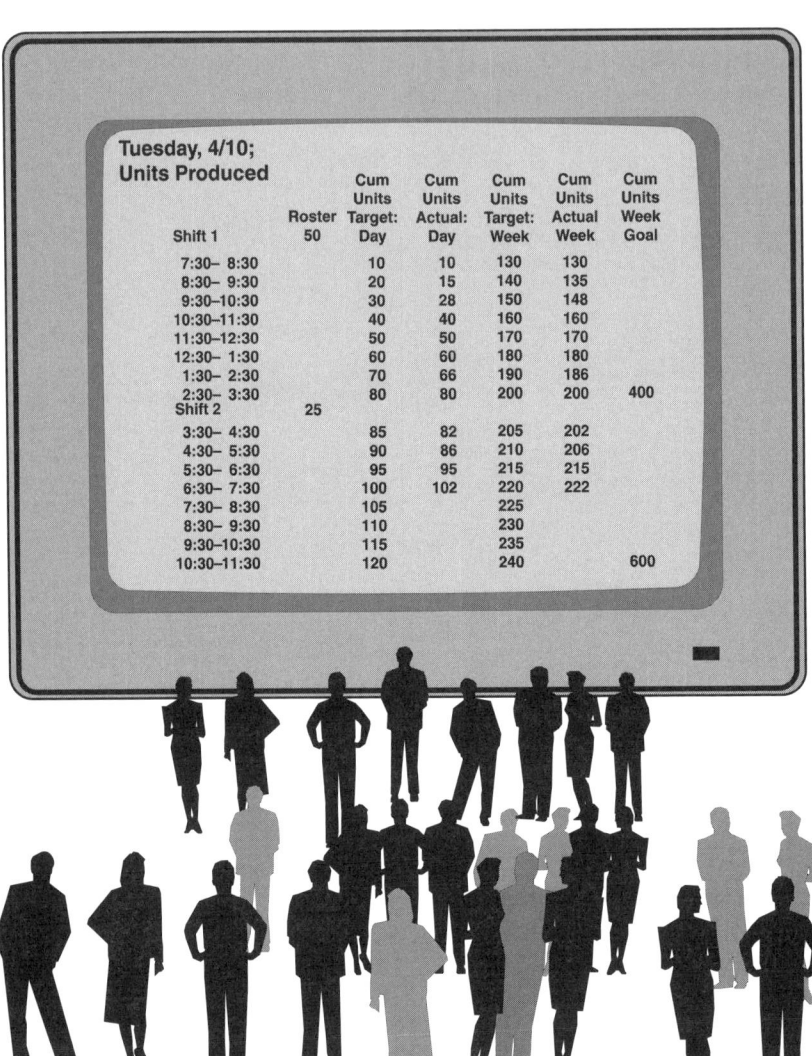

Tuesday, 4/10; Units Produced

Shift 1	Roster 50	Cum Units Target: Day	Cum Units Actual: Day	Cum Units Target: Week	Cum Units Actual Week	Cum Units Week Goal
7:30– 8:30		10	10	130	130	
8:30– 9:30		20	15	140	135	
9:30–10:30		30	28	150	148	
10:30–11:30		40	40	160	160	
11:30–12:30		50	50	170	170	
12:30– 1:30		60	60	180	180	
1:30– 2:30		70	66	190	186	
2:30– 3:30		80	80	200	200	400
Shift 2	25					
3:30– 4:30		85	82	205	202	
4:30– 5:30		90	86	210	206	
5:30– 6:30		95	95	215	215	
6:30– 7:30		100	102	220	222	
7:30– 8:30		105		225		
8:30– 9:30		110		230		
9:30–10:30		115		235		
10:30–11:30		120		240		600

CROSS-TRAINING MATRIX

An empowerment recipe collection favorite because it's so easy to prepare and can be used for technical and/or administrative tasks!

Ingredients
- 1 direct labor manufacturing team roster by service date within process
- 1 list of unit operations within team process

Makes one serving (for manufacturing)

1. Using a predetermined measure of history, derive each team member's average performance for each participated sequential unit operation within a process, product, or service that the team is responsible for. Performance measure should be based on some combination of selected criteria (quality, productivity, safety, attendance, housekeeping, experience, etc.).
2. Set standards of superior and acceptable performance for each sequential unit operation. The latter becomes a baseline for each team member's training decision.
3. For each sequential unit operation, identify an expert qualified by superior performance (above). Tab expert as the trainer for that specific unit operation. Let stand.

    If no team member qualifies as a superior performer/expert, then other alternatives must be considered:
    - ✔ Team leader, coach, manager, manufacturing engineering, or training (pending expertise) serves role until a team member qualifies.
    - ✔ External training expertise is hired and serves role until a team member qualifies.
4. Identify team members who, based on performance history versus acceptable performance standard, will not have to be trained for specific unit operations.
5. Determine service date within process for each rostered team member.
6. Communicate to the team the intent to implement a cross training plan. Highlight concept of performance-based

experts/trainers, performance standard qualifiers, performance data measured during training, and service date within process priority. Reinforce requirement that until an acceptable performance standard is achieved for a specific unit operation, no team member will be allowed to perform that task.
7. Simmer, soliciting input as to acceptance and/or refinement.
8. Mix in team input relative to the amount of training time required to achieve an acceptable performance standard. Stir in input as to the amount of time/chances allowable for maintaining an acceptable performance standard before retraining is required. Reach consensus.
9. Construct a cross training matrix with columnar headings of team member, process service date, and sequential unit operations. Under team member, list all rostered employees sequenced by longest accrued service date within process. For each sequential unit operation, identify the anticipated training start and completion date using service date as a priority. Begin with the longest accrued service employee, targeting their training in the first sequenced unit operation that they have not been trained in or achieved an acceptable performance standard at the time of implementing the cross training plan. (Note: The cross training plan will probably be subjected to constant changes and reiterations because of schedule conflicts, absenteeism, vacations, other priorities, and so forth. Also, members that fail to achieve an acceptable standard of performance during training will be placed last in training sequence priority for that specific unit operation, allowing for a complete pass of all other team members needing that particular training prior to a subsequent attempt. Additionally, retraining for not maintaining an acceptable performance standard also results in being placed last in the training priority sequence.)
10. Post cross-training matrix in visible team location(s).

Variation
Add a formal certification process that may include rigid guidelines relative to performance, performance maintenance, audits, and an accumulation of points for achieving skill competency of successive unit operations. Blend in a pay-for-skills component or some derivative thereof to sustain momentum and increase motivation.

Tip
For increased awareness and commitment, involve the team in constructing, updating, and posting the cross training matrix. The champion's goal will be to eventually turn ownership of the process over to the team. Now you're cooking!

Sample Cross-Training Matrix

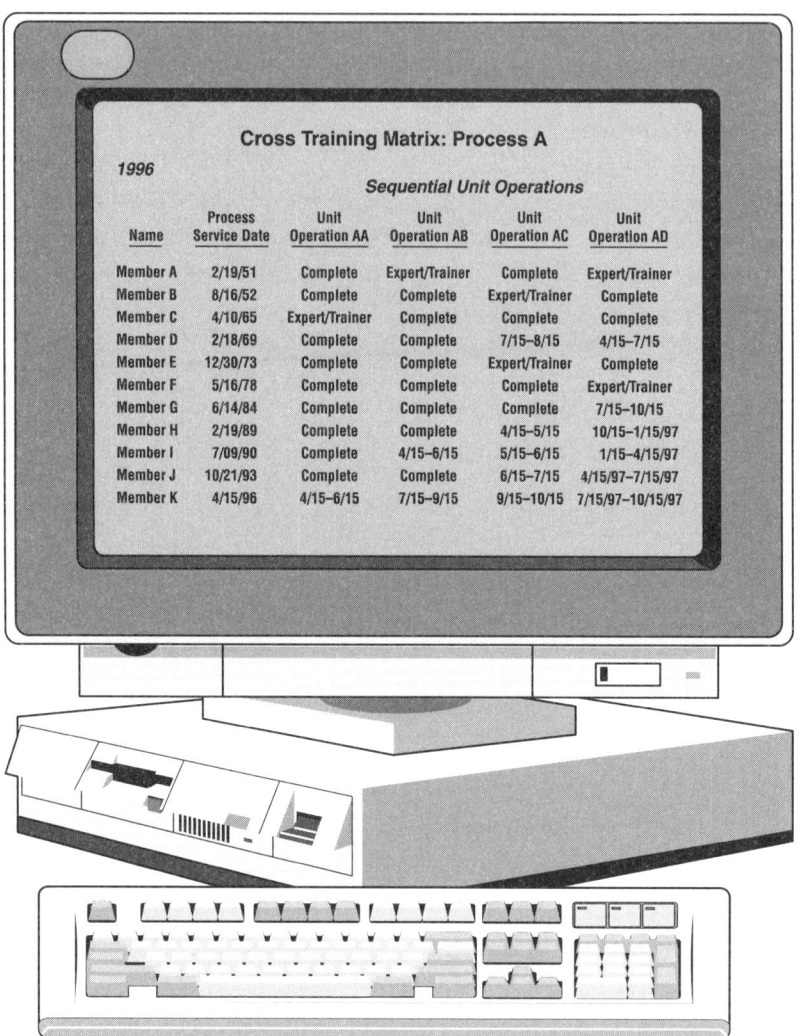

CO-LOCATION

Stir development and manufacturing engineering, materials, finance, management, marketing, customer service, and/or business team representation into the mix for added color and flavor. Makes for a great stew!

Ingredients
    1 nonmanufacturing product, process, project, or service team
    1 vision
    1 mission
    goals

Makes one serving (for nonmanufacturing)

1. Physically co-locate team members. Having team members sit side by side greatly enhances their communication, fosters commitment, and provides the capacity to focus on quick response!
2. Facilitate a daily review of progress against goals; carve out actions to resolve roadblocks or issues.
3. Meanwhile, provide frequent information flow of team's progress to sponsors and/or team member's functional management; this will greatly reduce anxiety for the latter over geographical displacement and assimilate performance feedback.
4. Serve.

Variation
Substitute frequent (daily) team conference calls for co-location if the latter is not possible from a distance or space constraint.

Tip
Co-location will promote a greater awareness of the big picture in getting the job done. Encourage a sharing of information and an understanding of each team member's role.

Sample Co-Location

Office Layout

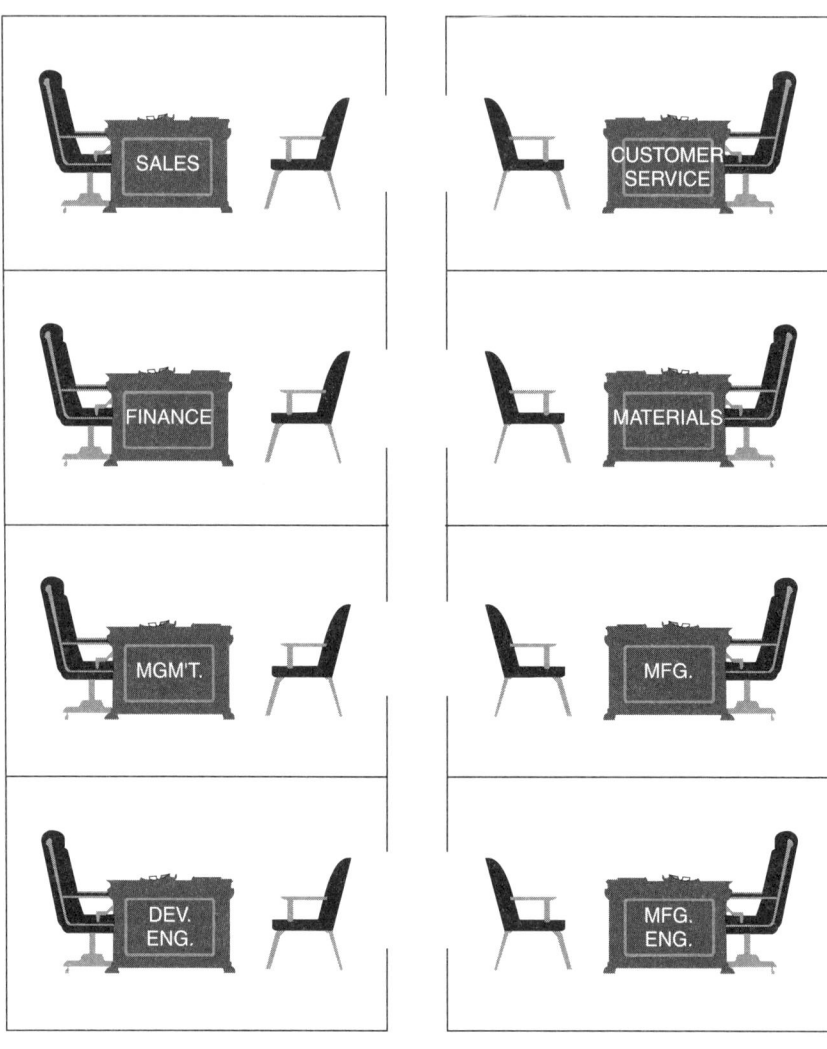

FUNCTIONAL PARITY

Almost any combination of team members can be used. It's a terrific way to complement the co-location dish!

Ingredients
>   1 nonmanufacturing product, process, project, or service team
>   1 vision
>   1 mission
>   goals

Makes one serving (for nonmanufacturing)

1. Involve all team members from the beginning of the process to the end.
2. Keep all team members on the same level of importance, because each will contribute essential ingredients to the cooking process. Co-location will reinforce parity!
3. Facilitate a common understanding of the importance of each team member's contribution to the success of the mission. Validate during the daily review of goals. Stir often.
4. Encourage a rotation of tasks that are general in nature (i.e., administrative).
5. Maintain at low heat.

Variation
Blend in a rotation (daily or weekly) of team members to facilitate the goal review process.

Tip
Beware: hand-offs destroy momentum! Enthusiasm developed by the original team cannot easily be transferred to successors.

Sample Functional Parity

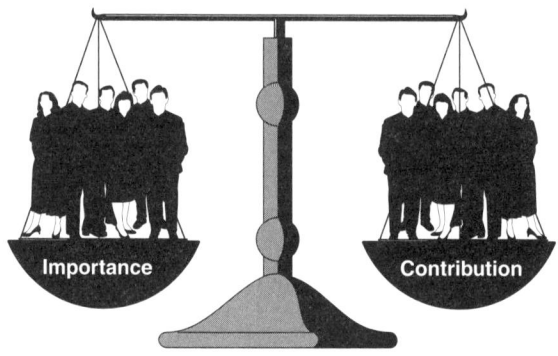

Considerations:

1. Do you feel as if your contributions are valued by the team?

2. Do you value the contributions of all team members?

3. Do team members solicit your ideas, comments, and/or feedback at a level of frequency or need that you are satisfied with?

4. Do you solicit ideas, comments, and/or feedback at a level of frequency that satisfies others?

5. Are you supportive and responsive to team member work needs?

6. Are team members responsive and supportive of your work needs?

7. Do you participate in team tasks outside of the area of your functional expertise?

BENCHMARKING

Best practice is the base for this fast-fixin' dish! Turn to this versatile serving when not sure what to serve or how to serve, or simply as a measure against the best.

Ingredients
    Selective subject matter literature
    Seminars/workshops
    Internal/external best practice empowered teams

Makes one serving (for manufacturing or nonmanufacturing)

1. Pare subject matter literature to selective topics relevant to team issues and concerns, or as positive reinforcement for progress made. (A valuable first step in benchmarking is to research subject matter literature to learn, compare, and measure against real case histories, alternative thinking, and/or documented performance from other organizations, teams, and/or businesses.)
2. Meanwhile, arrange for team and/or representatives to attend appropriate seminars/workshops to continue learnings, sustain focus, and network. (Sending teams and/or representatives to relevant seminars/workshops provides visible access to subject matter experts or those that have experienced change.)
3. Mix in site visits to internal/external best practice empowered teams. Best practice teams representing similar product, process, or service add a hearty flavor! (Site visits present an opportunity to observe and dialogue with the best. I've always felt that if you return with a minimum of a single lesson learned, then the site visit served a purpose!)
4. Maintain low heat, stirring often.

Variation
Substitute telephone exchange or surveys to best practice teams for benchmarking, if the cost of travel or time away from work is prohibitive or impractical.

Tip
Engaging the team in benchmarking generates enthusiasm, especially seminars/workshops and site visits; seeing is believing!

Sample Benchmarking

Information Search   Seminars/Workshops   Internal/External Site Visits

Company/ Metrics	External Best Practice	Internal Best Practice	Team Performance	Team Better/Worse
Company A				
• Time to market.	14 weeks	**10 weeks**	13 weeks	(30.0%)
• Product cost.	**$3,350**	$3,400	$3,500	(4.5%)
• Quality level (sigma).	5.6 sigma	5.7 sigma	**5.8 sigma**	1.8%
• Number of parts.	**90**	100	115	(27.8%)
• Number of suppliers	43	48	**36**	19.4%
• Engineering change orders (ECOs) per proj.	**5**	6	8	(60.0%)
Company B				
• Unit weight.	**8 kilograms**	12 kilograms	10 kilograms	(25.0%)
• Delivery cycle time.	**10 hours**	13 hours	18 hours	(80.0%)
• Reuse of parts (%).	35%	25%	**42%**	20.0%
• Manufacturing cost (%).	**19%**	33%	28%	(47.4%)
Company C				
• Early supplier involvement (ESI).	Yes	Yes	Yes	Parity
• Time to market as % of cycle time.	**33%**	39%	43%	(30.3%)

CUSTOMER VISITS

Listen to the voice of the customer—for what customers say will give you a better idea of their tastes. Serve a product, process, or service to their satisfaction and delight; they will be back for more!

Ingredients
>Internal customers
>External customers

Makes one serving (for manufacturing or nonmanufacturing)

1. Arrange for frequent (daily/weekly) internal customer interface; identify/anticipate customer needs to produce customer delight.
2. Meanwhile, increase level of external customer sensitivity using customer site visits, focus groups, telephone calls, customer satisfaction surveys, customer complaint letters, as voice-of-the-customer tools. An excellent means of analyzing customer requirements and deploying them into business operations is quality functional deployment. (Quality functional deployment (QFD) is a system of new product development that helps development engineers determine what customer needs are and translates those needs into design requirements. The intent is to let product design be driven by the voice of the customer, not the voice of engineering. The system uses a chart that resembles a drawing of a house and is frequently referred to as the house of quality. In a QFD chart, customer desires (derived from tools mentioned above) are grouped by category and written along the vertical axis of the array. Product characteristics are written across the top, while the matrix checks correlations. An excellent reference on the subject with detailed methodology for using this approach is the book *The Roadmap to Repeatable Success, Using QFD to Implement Change*, by Barbara A. Bicknell and Kris D. Bicknell.)
3. Prepare a database of customer's environments, applications, and unmet needs; update regularly.

4. Serve product, process, and/or service improvements resulting from customer inputs.

Variation
Add customer representation to problem-solving teams, project teams, and flash meetings (internal customers).

Tip
Team or team member interface with internal/external customers will increase awareness of product, process, or service application by customer, heighten sensitivity to customer needs, and instill ownership of the whole piece of work!

Customer Visits

Sample Customer Visits

Complaints

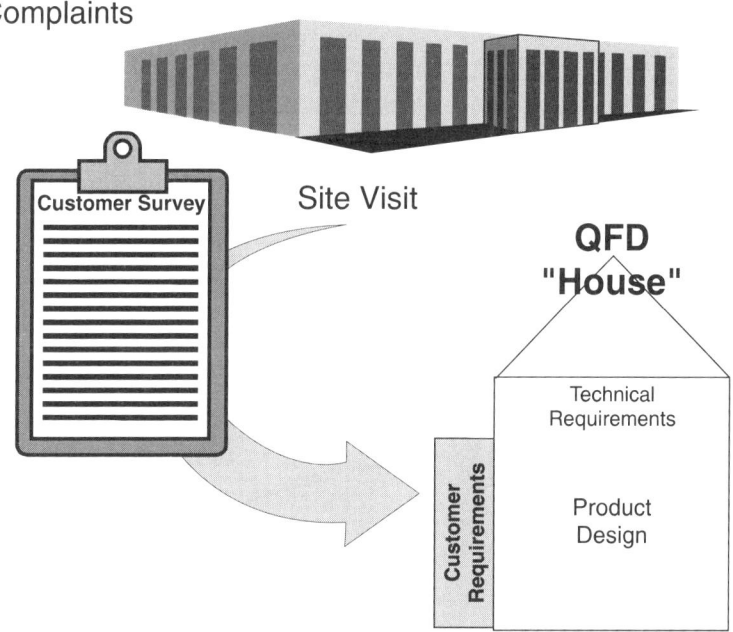

Site Visit

Empowerment Process Model
Preheat Elements

Manufacturing Recipes:

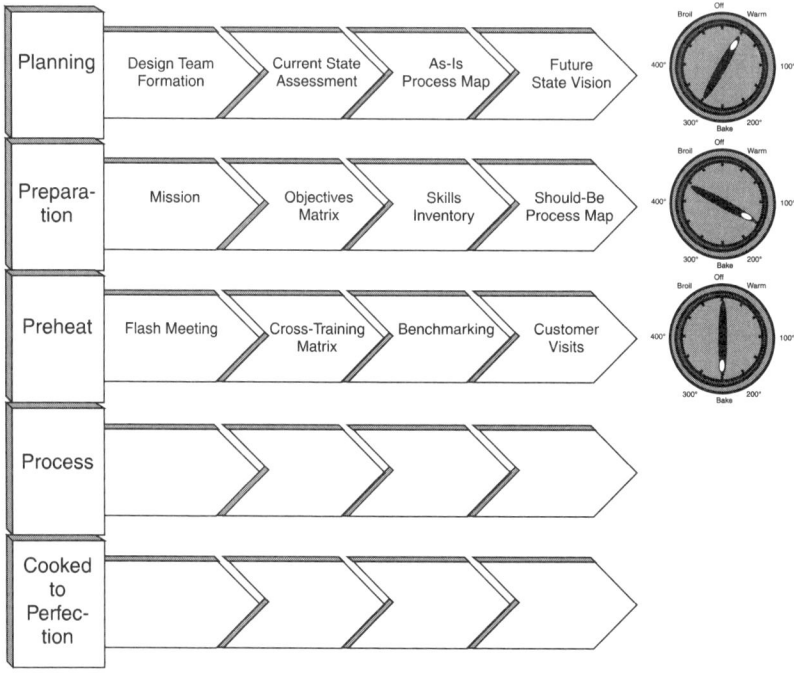

Empowerment Process Model
Preheat Elements

Nonmanufacturing Recipes:

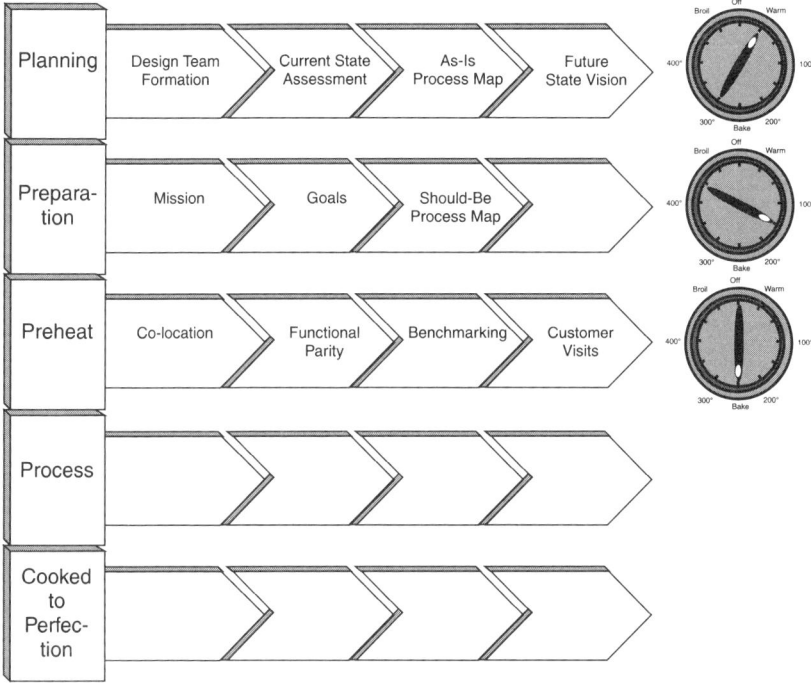

SUMMARY

The key to a successful change strategy is the involvement of many. Your task as Champion of Empowered Organizations during the preheat stage is to do just that. The amount of time that you will spend organizing, facilitating, and even scrambling from team to team will test your stamina and resolve. Make every attempt to be there for every meeting as this is a critical stage for sustaining momentum, garnering support, and reinforcing that this is not just another program that will fade. Some will look for inconsistency; you have to be consistent!

Preheat is the warming element that creates an atmosphere of teamwork and participation. Dialogue, as both an ingredient and an outcome, will be a factor in each team's successful transition to the next stage of the process. Aside from facilitating that dialogue, teams will assume that you are the product, process, or service expert by virtue of your champion's role. Unless your credentials can validate that claim, clarify that assumption; your credibility could be at risk as time passes! Remember, they are the functional experts; draw from them the need, the desire, and the actions to improve and change. That is a champion's challenge!

Involving the team in benchmarking-recognized best-practice teams will provide an opportunity to gauge progress, learn from experience, and set the standard for which to reach. Never stop or become complacent with success, especially when you become best practice.

Finally, listen to the voice of the customer. They keep us in business! Serve a product, process, or service that produces total customer satisfaction.

The change strategy is now baking; the temperature of the organization is climbing!

PART FOUR

PROCESS

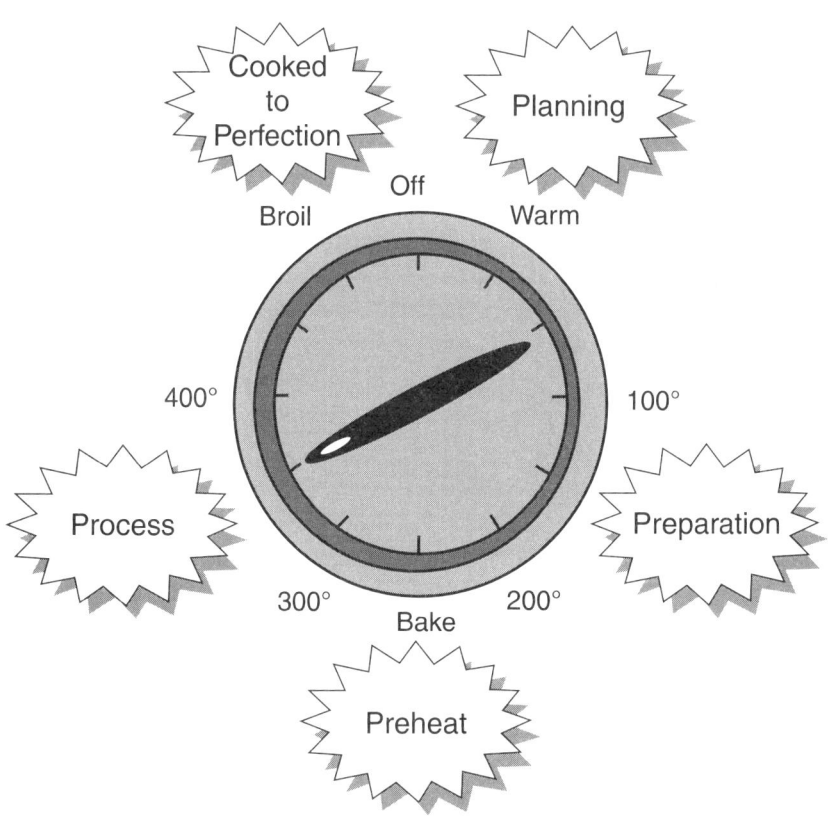

PROCESS

The "Process" part of this book is filled with delicious recipes that are so enticing they'll ensure that empowerment remains as the most desired change strategy. Champions and teams alike will find the rich and flavorful context of empowerment both refreshing and satisfying as the organization continues to bake!

The process element begins with the rollout of a well developed communication strategy intended to inform the organization or business of impending changes. Make sure that communication is timely and frequent; you will gain buy-in and support, and remember that there aren't many that like surprises!

The next step in the process element is job redesign. The intent here is to redesign jobs with the understanding that team members will share joint responsibility for performing the whole piece of work. When you redesign jobs that are value-added and motivating, realign information flow, and add decision-making capability, the outcome is ownership!

Information sharing is crucial for teams in understanding the performance challenge, as well as in grasping the reason for higher level decisions. With access to the same information, management and employees are more likely to collaborate in the change effort and build trust.

For manufacturing, as teams become more flexible in job assignment, participate in decision making, solve problems, and improve overall performance, traditional compensation practices become outdated. Champions and teams will need to evolve and advocate pay practices based upon skills and team performance. Team-based pay mixed with various recognition programs will serve as reinforcement for the team concept, instill pride, be highly motivating, and enable personal development and career growth.

For nonmanufacturing, although team-based compensation practices are a viable alternative, it has been my experience that job specialization, the dynamics of project assignment, and project duration make it less likely or more difficult to implement. It is more likely that various reward programs geared toward project completion measures or milestone achievement are more appropriate; supplemented with various types of recognition, reward programs have a motivating effect.

You are now ready to select the process recipes that will continue the empowerment journey. Patience is key as the baking time will be the longest stage of the change strategy. Everyone is getting excited as the final product is about to be served!

COMMUNICATION STRATEGY

Substitute a variety of communication types for the same delicious results. A well-balanced and nutritional serving that complements a change strategy nicely!

Ingredients

    Memorandum   Displays
    Newsletters   Home mailings
    Department meetings   Flyers
    Focus groups   E-mail
    Banners   Informal dialogue
    Videos   Briefings

Makes one serving (for manufacturing or nonmanufacturing)

1. Develop a communication strategy to inform the balance of the organization or business of current or intended change effort activities. (Communication of any major organizational change requires that the message get through to employees to enlist their support, cooperation, and involvement. However, how you communicate can help or hinder the change effort! It is worth remembering that traditional organizations have an established hierarchical relationship between frontline employees and first-line supervision. Targeting first-line supervision as key receivers will go a long way in winning their support and in having them bring the rest of the employees with them. As the organization evolves through the change process and behaviors are changed and structural relationships dismantled, communication as a direct link to frontline employees will become the norm.)

2. Test communication strategy with sponsors, unions (if applicable), and other organization members to gain insight into acceptance and/or refinement. Mix until smooth.

3. Seek legal counsel relative to communication context. Shape an aggregate communication strategy.

4. Serve often.

Variation
Communicate new expectations of performance by comparison to competing companies or by making internal company comparisons, rather than by vision alone.

Tip
In traditional organizations, employee attitude surveys frequently and predictably say that communications are poor; be conscious of that! Make communications frequently and timely, and mix in various types to keep the organization or business well informed, involved, and enthused. Any form of communication strategy provides information and value to a change process. It is my opinion that half-day or full-day change forums comprised of panel discussions and speakers are the most effective. A mix of senior management with external subject matter experts (consultants, authors, and/or practitioners) can create an informative and motivating program.

Sample Communication Strategy

JOB REDESIGN

Serve an assortment of multidimensional jobs to add pizzazz to the change strategy. If you like, stir in an array of task choices and decision making capability—that's how most employees enjoy their work!

Ingredients
    1 whole piece of work
    1 future state vision
    1 mission statement
    1 should-be process map
    1 as-is process map
    Relevant information

Makes one serving (for manufacturing or nonmanufacturing)

1. Restructure a team as a unit that naturally falls together to do a whole piece of work, grouping specialists and generalists alike. Co-location serves this purpose well.
2. Review the team's future state vision and mission as a reminder of the compelling reason(s) for change. (Continue to reference the vision as a yardstick for measuring the progress of the redesign effort. Raise the question as to whether the results of redesign match the vision. If so, then redesign is making progress. If not, then more effort or refinement is required.)
3. Meanwhile, reference the should-be process map to focus on the team's ideal future conversion process. Note boundary shifts from the team's current conversion process as depicted in the as-is process map. (If should-be or as-is process maps have not been completed, complete them before moving to the next step.)
4. Focusing on boundary shifts defined by the should-be process map, eliminate the non-value-adding work that exists because of boundaries within the as-is structure and to compensate for process fragmentation.

5. Redesign jobs with the premise that team members will share joint responsibility for performing the whole piece of work in the team's ideal conversion process. (Team assignments should have equal significance and desirability upon redesign.)
6. Meanwhile, carve out the various types of information that the team will need access to for problem solving and assessing performance. Mix in vigorously.
7. Design in the responsibility and freedom to make decisions within the boundaries of the team.
8. Serve hot or cold.

Variation
Job redesign can best be accomplished by the participation of empowered team members, facilitated by the Champion of Empowered Organizations and/or design team members. However, an alternate approach would be to have the redesign effort conducted by an internal redesign team or external consultants.

Tip
A well-designed job is one that begins at the upper limits of one's talents, then demands expansion of those talents!

Sample Job Redesign

Before Job Redesign:

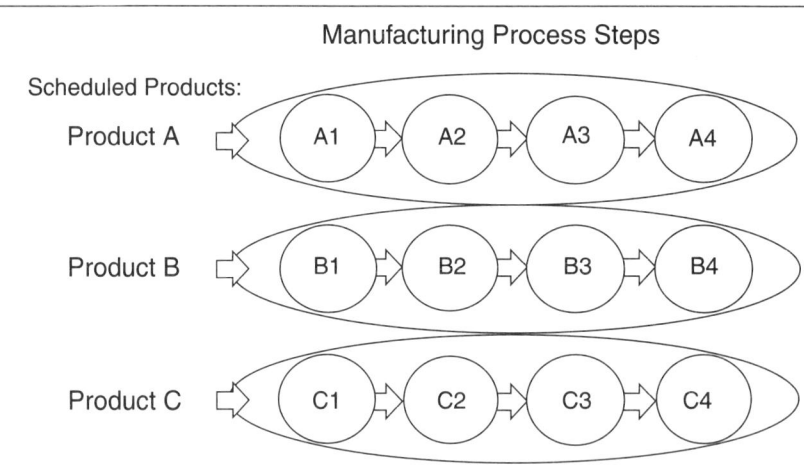

A functionally designed manufacturing operation before redesign.

Under the functional design, products A, B, and C are released to manufacturing and processed by functionally skilled labor. Priority issues, delays, and nonlinear flows are experienced.

After Job Redesign:

A team-based manufacturing operation after redesign.

Product A, B, and C schedules are released to manufacturing teams that are cross-trained in all four process steps. Priority issues and/or delays nonexistent or minimal, and linear flows result. Teams take responsibility for whole product.

INFORMATION SHARING

Delicious when served hot! It's a terrific way to add spice to a performance challenge, a change strategy, or just to understand higher level decisions.

Ingredients
> Key business information
> Performance feedback
> Communications
> Assimilation and departure information and feedback from incoming and exiting team members

Makes one serving (for manufacturing or nonmanufacturing)

1. Provide team access to information relevant to understanding and/or making decisions for necessary improvement to team performance, individual performance, organizational performance, and the performance of the company.
2. Provide data-based objective feedback (positive and/or negative) relative to performance (above).
3. Meanwhile, mix in information specific to overall business issues, successes, and short-term and long-term objectives.
4. Provide team access to information relevant to understanding and/or for the purpose of making decisions for needed changes in the workplace (processes, equipment, structure, etc.).
5. Add key business information related to competitive strategy and financial performance. Mix as necessary for making key decisions necessary for goal achievement, organizational alignment, and environmental satisfaction.
6. Serve and partner in improving performance, competitive position, and increasing trust, responsibility, and accountability.

Variation
Substitute a well-designed team system for gathering information, processing, and decision making in lieu of providing or seeking information on a need-to-know or performance correction basis only.

Tip
Increased information sharing will extend responsibility for results to lower levels of the organization. Teams/employees need to understand the potential consequences of poor decisions; in time, they will only have themselves to blame—or praise!

Sample Information Sharing

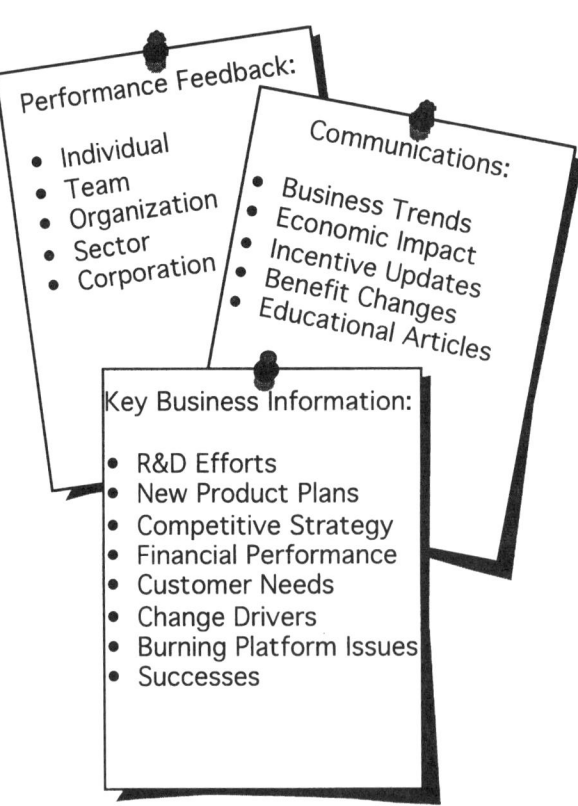

Performance Feedback:
- Individual
- Team
- Organization
- Sector
- Corporation

Communications:
- Business Trends
- Economic Impact
- Incentive Updates
- Benefit Changes
- Educational Articles

Key Business Information:
- R&D Efforts
- New Product Plans
- Competitive Strategy
- Financial Performance
- Customer Needs
- Change Drivers
- Burning Platform Issues
- Successes

TEAM-BASED PAY/RECOGNITION

Be creative with the condiments: use contribution and performance as the base for compensation. For added flavor, sprinkle in an assortment of recognition programs.

Ingredients
    1 Champion of Empowered Organizations
    1 design team
    Representatives from compensation, human resources, legal, and union(s), if applicable
    Assorted recognition programs

Makes one serving (for manufacturing)

1. Collaborate on creating and implementing good systems of performance measurement. The objectives matrix serves well as a good team performance measurement system. Mix with traditional leadership point system evaluations of individual performance, gradually evolving into peer reviews or some combination of the approaches.
2. Structure a compensation program that links base pay to team performance. (A number of nontraditional compensation systems are being adopted by a growing number of companies. Gain-sharing, pay-for-knowledge, lump-sum bonuses, a mix of team performance-based pay systems, and two-tier plans continue to surface and be implemented. Considerable literature addresses the concerns that drive companies to adopt major changes in compensation practices, as well as to define the context of the various types. One book in particular does a good job of articulating the pay challenge: *Workplace 2000*, by Joseph H. Boyett and Henry P. Conn; it will serve you well as a reference. A practical approach that has proved effective in my experience is to incorporate elements of individual and team performance into base pay, gradually increasing team impact percentage. For example, a 20/80 (20 percent team/80 percent individual) program launch could change to splits of 30/70, 40/60,

50/50, and so on, in subsequent merit periods until reaching predesignated caps.)
3. Communicate with and educate manufacturing employees, teams, management, and sponsors on the team-based pay concept seeking input relative to design strengths and/or weaknesses. Accept/refine based on insight/suggestions received. Communicate each program refinement until consensus is reached and approval gained for implementation.
4. Mix in an assortment of individual and team recognition awards/programs. Examples include:
   - ✔ Employee of the month.
   - ✔ Peak performer.
   - ✔ Employee suggestion awards.
   - ✔ Team suggestion awards.
   - ✔ Cash/cash substitute/gift certificates.
   - ✔ Recognition plaques/trophies.
   - ✔ Time off.
   - ✔ Productivity/production/quality awards.
   - ✔ Attendance/safety/housekeeping awards.
5. Serve.

Variation
Substitute pay for knowledge or pay for skills as an alternate pay strategy within the team context.

Tip
Team-based pay launch is best served upon completion of the job redesign effort. Team-based pay will complement redesign and provide a degree of motivation in continuing and sustaining the empowerment journey. When launching team-based pay, you will find it beneficial to select or to ask teams to volunteer as "pilots" for rollout, in order to identify and correct for issues that may not have been anticipated during design.

Sample Team-Based Pay/Recognition

Team-Based Pay Context:

% Weighting

Team Performance Score:

- Desired weighting (e.g., 20%).

- Evaluated based on team results (e.g., objectives matrix).

- Team members involved in tracking results and developing process improvements.

% Weighting

Individual Performance Score:

- Behaviorally anchored rating (traditional point system evaluation).

- Based on organization performance factors.

- Desired weighting (e.g., 80%).

Sample Team-Based Pay/Recognition (concluded)

Team-Based Pay Context:

Overall Performance Score Comprises:

- Team score (20%).

- Individual score (80%).

Individual's Performance Score: Determines individual's pay within the range.

Overall Performance Score Influence on Pay:

1. Higher performing teams are eligible for a larger merit increase budget.

2. Overall performance score is used to determine annual merit increase.

REWARD AND RECOGNITION

All of our taste testers preferred this serving! Most any combination of programs can be used. It's a terrific way to use leftovers, too.

Ingredients
>1 Champion of Empowered Organizations
>1 design team
>Representatives from compensation, human resources, legal, and union(s), if applicable
>Assorted reward and recognition programs

Makes one serving (for nonmanufacturing)

1. Collaborate on creating, developing, and implementing good systems of individual and team performance measurement. Mix with existing performance systems that are relevant and effective.
2. Create and develop new reward and recognition programs that reflect changing individual and team performance systems. Add team input to mix.
3. Carve out, refine, and use as-is reward and recognition programs that are relevant and effective. Solicit team input as to program selection, enhancement, and motivation.
4. Test reward and recognition cost and application feasibility with sponsors, unions (if applicable), and other organization members to gain insight into acceptance and/or refinement. Mix until smooth.
5. Select a well balanced assortment of individual and team reward and recognition programs. Examples include:
   - ✔ Employee of the month.
   - ✔ Peak performer.
   - ✔ Milestone achievement bonuses, rewards, and/or recognition.
   - ✔ Cash/cash substitute/gift certificates.
   - ✔ Recognition plaques/trophies.
   - ✔ Time off.

Variation
Benchmark internal and external reward and recognition programs for application. Blend or add as appropriate and effective.

Tip
Active participation by teams in the design of reward and recognition programs will not be lacking as it is one of the more popular recipes. Reinforce, however, a balanced mix of individual and team programs and their alignment to improved business improvement.

Sample Reward and Recognition

Reward *worksheet* (to solicit team input):
1. What existing individual reward and recognition programs should continue to be used?

2. What existing team reward and recognition programs should continue to be used?

3. Are existing reward and recognition programs timely and specific?

4. What types of individual achievements and/or milestones should be rewarded and/or recognized?

5. What types of team achievements and/or milestones should be rewarded and/or recognized?

6. What types of reward and recognition programs will motivate team members to work together?

7. What types of reward and recognition programs will inspire individuals to excel?

8. What types of reward and recognition programs will inspire teams to excel?

9. What mix of individual and team reward and recognition programs should there be?

Empowerment Process Model
Process Elements

Manufacturing Recipes:

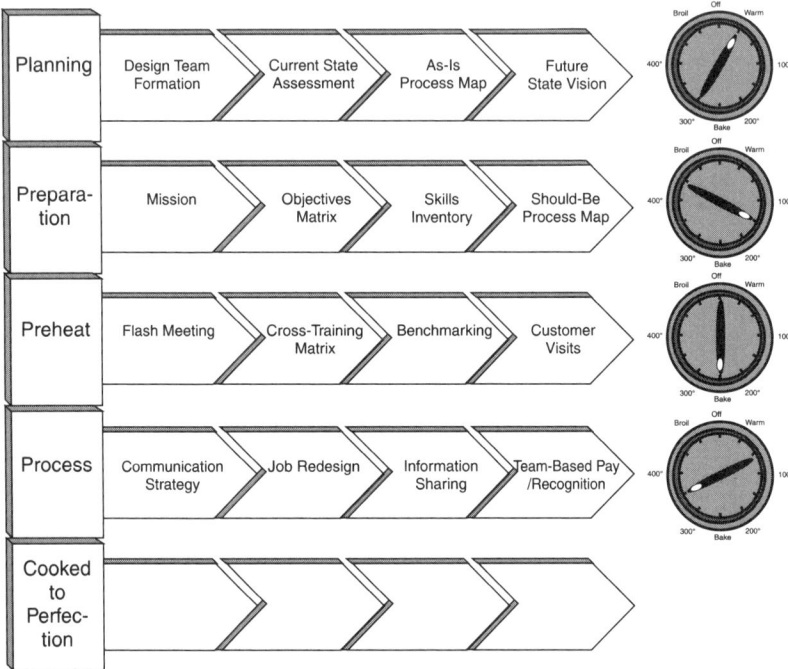

Empowerment Process Model
Process Elements

Nonmanufacturing Recipes:

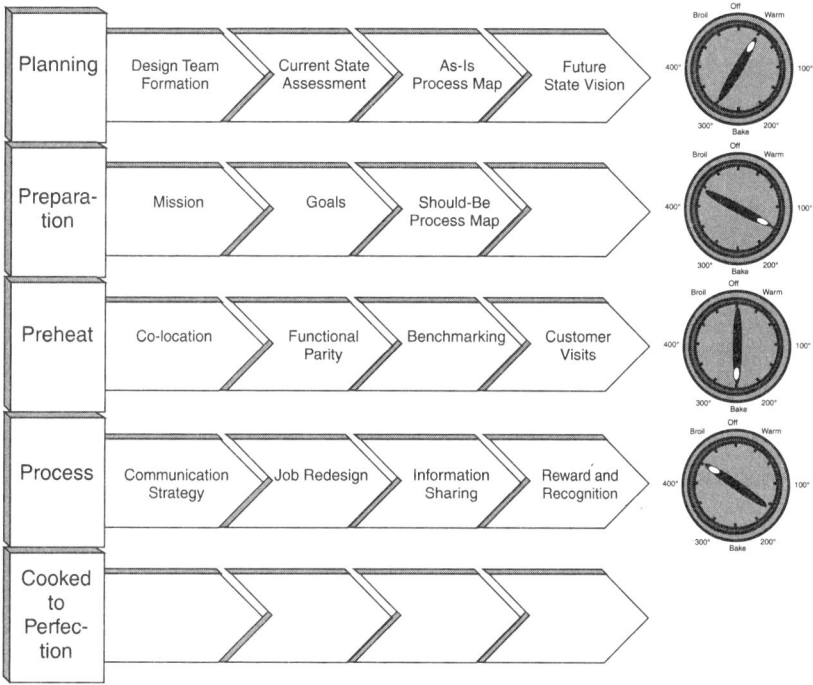

SUMMARY

Teamwork divides effort and multiplies the effect—this states the reality in all aspects of this change process. The process part of the journey, now complete, means that you have persevered and have leveraged the efforts of many people in planning and evolving a changing culture. The paradigm shift characterized by high commitment, high involvement, and empowerment is becoming a visible testimony to what a champion with desire and passion can accomplish. However, don't rest on these laurels just yet; there's more work to do!

Process is the baking element that creates a sense of accomplishment and energizes the team for the last leg of the journey. This stage is very difficult in terms of time and effort expended. Yet, who ever said that translating a vision into reality is easy? That is a champion's challenge and a measure of our success!

Communication is extremely important throughout the change process, but it is never so critical as it is in the process stage. Here the status quo becomes a culture of the past, while jobs, processes, and reward systems are redesigned for alignment to the vision. Developing and serving a sound communication strategy to inform the business or organization of current or intended changes will pay dividends in terms of support, understanding, and participation.

Redesigning jobs with the intent that team members will share joint responsibility for performing the whole piece of work in the team's ideal conversion process is at the very core of empowerment. Incorporating the responsibility and freedom to make decisions in the design process is essential to creating a sense of ownership and autonomy.

Realignment of information systems to create information sharing will facilitate the capability for making decisions within the team structure. Seek information that is pertinent to improving team performance and for understanding higher level decisions, competitive strategy, and financial results. Don't be surprised if some information is difficult to get—keep after it!

Structuring a compensation system that links base pay to team performance is critical in sustaining momentum, especially for manufacturing. Having a team-based organization operating with classic individual performance and compensation systems will be in direct conflict. A good team performance measurement system will serve as a catalyst for making changes in the mechanics of compensation. Expectations have already been set for such a change. Timing is critical!

Reward and recognition programs add flavor to the change process. Any assortment is preferred. Programs oriented to results or behavior and developed and/or implemented by teams or team members will have a positive impact on morale and performance. Challenge their creativity; the dividends will be significant!

The process stage is now complete; the organization is ready to cook to perfection!

PART FIVE

COOKED TO PERFECTION

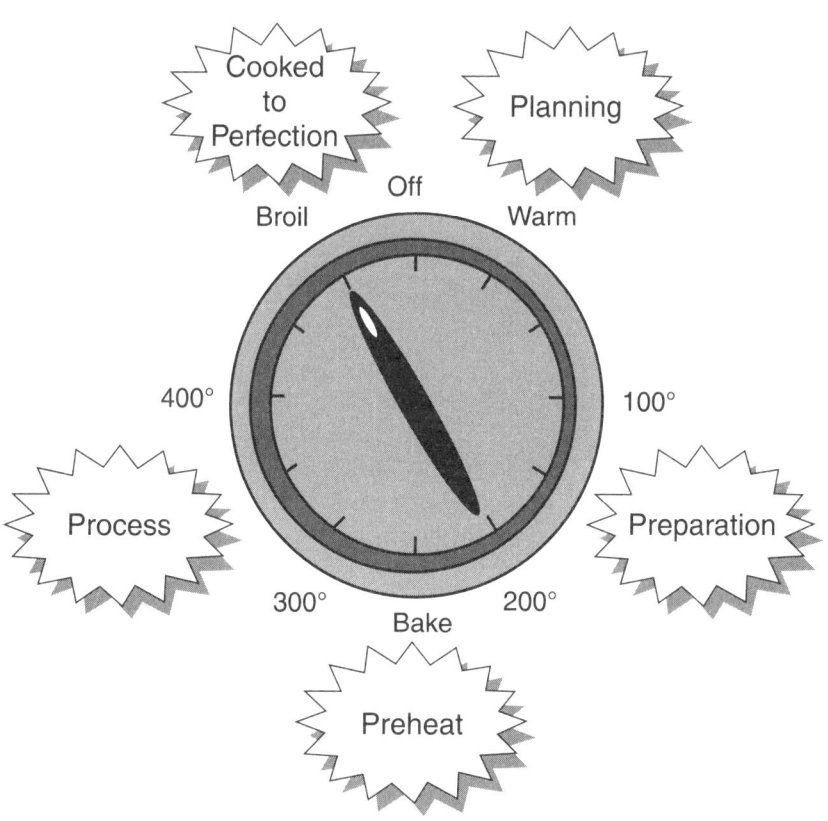

COOKED TO PERFECTION

The luscious recipes in this chapter fit all the expectations that empowerment embodies and are so inviting that the organization will cook to perfection for a long time! Both champions and teams will savor the increased capability of the organization to move rapidly and effectively to satisfy customers. Empowerment is truly the foundation for performance improvement and increased organizational capability!

The cooked-to-perfection stage begins with transition, the journey from the current state to the future state. It is a road traveled by many, but successfully navigated by few. The key to a successful transition is to develop a road map of empowerment design actions for each stage of the process model. Be task specific, identify champions, and drive toward a targeted completion date. It will also be imperative to secure the active support and involvement of those who will ensure that change will take place. Above all, remember to communicate the intent, impact, and outcome of change actions to everyone!

The next step in the cooked-to-perfection stage is the alignment of organizational systems. If not properly aligned, in-place organizational systems will work to counter empowered team implementation. Identify, modify, and/or design new systems that will promote the empowerment initiative and team-based structure. The alignment of business goals from top to bottom of the organizational hierarchy is also a critical element. Team goals need to correlate to the business results desired by the organization.

Developing a partnership between employees/teams, management, and union(s) is a formidable challenge, but a desired relationship and outcome of empowerment. Collaboration in defining competitive strategy, goal setting, decision making, and visioning will lead to mutual understanding, commitment, and ownership. Sharing successes and failures will also promote a cohesive team-based structure and partnership.

Finally, renewal will create the capacity to determine whether the current empowered team design is appropriate in the wake of changes from an updated environmental scan or a change in competitive strategy. Revitalization plans or developing a new vision will sustain the momentum.

You are now ready to select the cooked-to-perfection recipes that will continue the empowerment journey. Put on your chef's hat; you are about to serve the organization the entree it has been waiting for!

TRANSITION

A favorite in all change agent kitchens! We serve it at all types of get-togethers and for communication strategies. Made at the height of the empowerment design process, it's especially great for management, sponsors, and union(s) as an appetizer for what lies directly ahead. For those of us who bake frequently, experience will lead to adding a variety of ingredients for more zip!

Ingredients
>1 current state assessment
>1 as-is process map
>1 future state vision
>1 should-be process map
>Change strategy actions

Makes one serving (for manufacturing or nonmanufacturing)

1. Develop a road map for the change effort that is meaningful, task specific, and time sequenced. Comparing the current state to the ideal future state as defined by the should-be process map, identify the specific action(s) at each process model stage that will be required for implementation.
2. Carve out the specific person(s), committees, or teams who will champion developing and implementing the specific action(s) required.
3. For each action, determine and list a required completion date.
4. Elicit the active support, involvement, and approval of management, sponsors, and union(s) in executing actions. Modify (pull in or delay) desired completion dates that result from the timing of organizational acceptance. Simmer.
5. Serve hot.

Variation
Substitute any action plan template that is preferred or generic to your team, organization, or business.

Tip
It is extremely important to assess the effect and/or progress of the change effort. Pending the outcome of the assessment, you may need to develop a plan to gain commitment from, or influence, the critical mass, management, sponsors, and/or union(s) if sponsorship, for whatever reason, has waned since the planning phase.

Sample Transition Plan

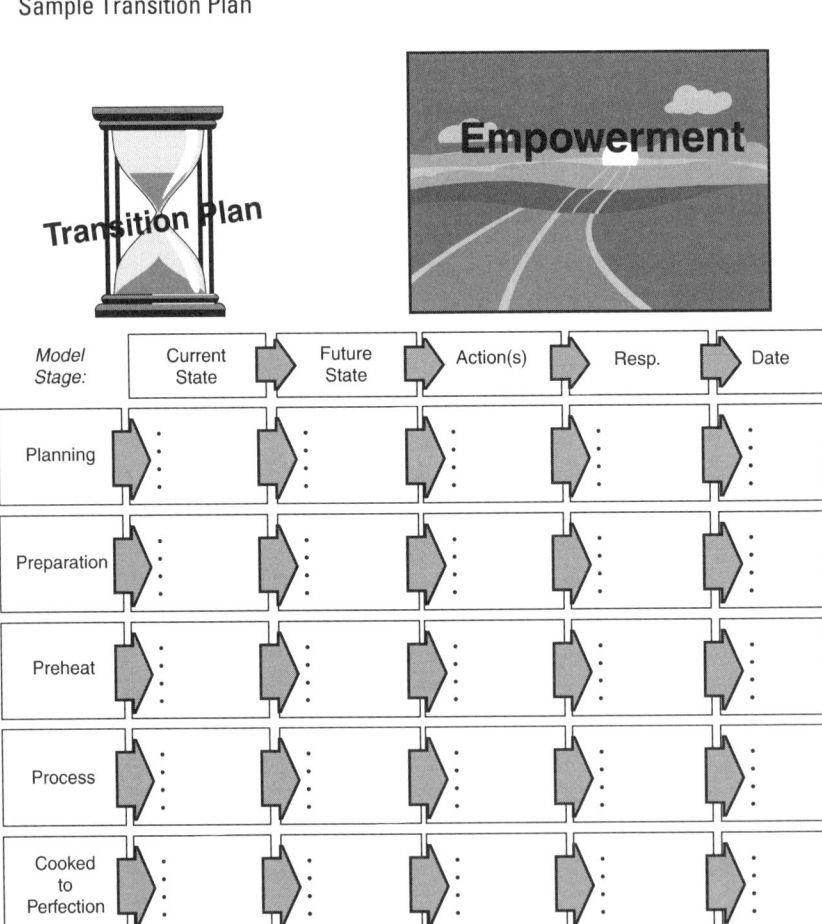

ALIGNMENT

Popular as a delicious topping to any empowerment serving. Try it over an array of organizational systems, as well as a hierarchy of business goals. A favorite in our empowerment kitchens!

Ingredients

    Various organizational systems:
    Human resource management:
- Performance management
- Selection and promotion
- Job assignment

    Information systems
    Technology
    Organizational structure
    Reward and recognition
    Labor relations
    Strategic and long-range planning
    Standards and measures
    Communication
    Training and development
    Budgeting
    Physical facilities
    External suppliers
    Business goals

Makes one serving (for manufacturing or nonmanufacturing)

1. Identify organizational systems that need to be in alignment for the empowerment strategy and team-based structure to operate as desired.
2. For each organizational system, question whether that system promotes or deters the empowerment initiative. If it deters empowerment, then rethink and redesign in-place organizational systems or design new ones to support new team values and behaviors.

3. Meanwhile, continue to monitor, analyze, and align organizational systems to promote optimal team performance.
4. Review and align, if necessary, business goals developed by the team with business results desired by the organization.
5. Serve.

Variation
There is benefit to aligning organizational systems prior to launching the empowerment change strategy, but experience indicates that it is unlikely. It can be more effective to focus on alignment early and throughout the change initiative to support and reinforce the desired outcome.

Tip
Lack of organizational alignment will create mixed messages, cause confusion, and undermine the empowerment change strategy. When organizational systems are aligned, new team values and behaviors are reinforced!

Alignment

Sample Alignment

Base Pay

Before Alignment:

After Alignment:

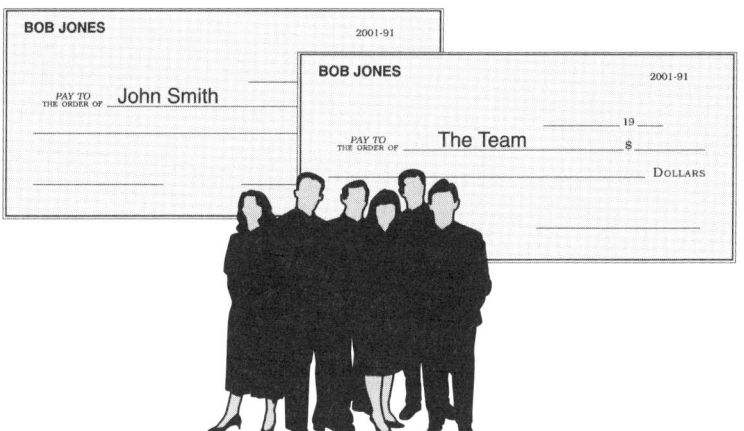

PARTNERSHIP

A great recipe for today's busy and healthy lifestyle! Tastes good when served with any or all of your empowerment fixings.

Ingredients
    Empowered teams
    Management hierarchy
    Union(s), if applicable
    Vision
    Goals
    Information sharing
    Reward and recognition

Makes one serving (for manufacturing or nonmanufacturing)

1. Develop visions at both the organization and team levels to depict the interrelationships and dependence for mutual success. Bake evenly.
2. Communicate the priority business goals of the organization that teams must support to achieve desired results. Add executive and management communication setting forth the reasons for the goals and the impact on financial performance and competitive strategy that goal achievement will effect. Add until message has desired consistency.
3. Involve everyone in the goal setting process. Set goals that are aligned with and support organizational priorities.
4. Create collaborative employee/management action plans to achieve desired outcomes.
5. Reinforce the need to share information. Mix the good news with the bad news. Blend, stopping frequently to assess any collaborative action necessary for corrective action or to continue achieving desired outcomes.
6. Carve out decision-making boundaries between teams and the management hierarchy, understanding that all critical organizational decisions can't be made outside of

the team scope; collaborate when alignment supports the decision making process for those instances.
7. Share in the rewards of organizational success and reward desired behaviors.
8. Partner.

Variation
Information sharing will drive responsibility for results lower in the organization. As rewards are shared for organizational success, teams will necessarily share the accountability for less-than-desired performance, as well.

Tip
Partnership manifests itself in many ways through behaviors, values, and systems. Reinforcing partnership will require significant energy in coaching, modeling, and training. Remember that success is a product of collaboration!

Sample Partnership

Before Partnership

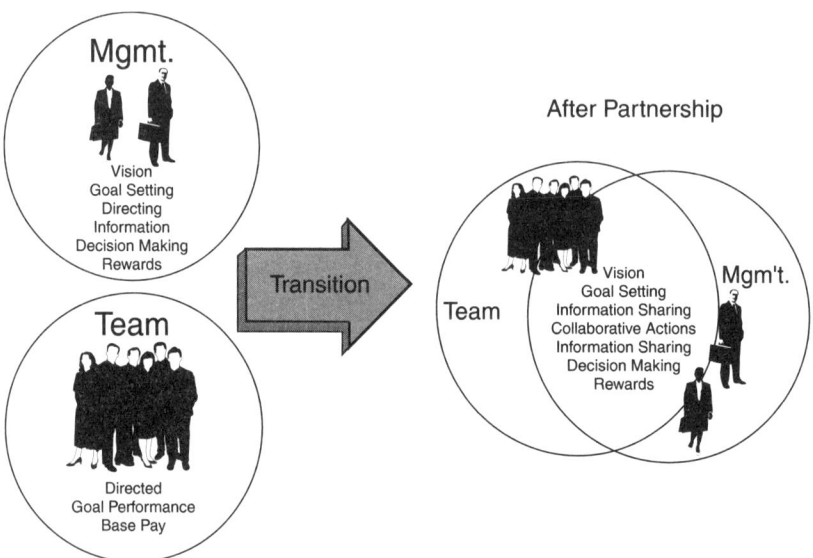

RENEWAL

This recipe truly lives up to its name. Before empowerment, this was quite a chore to make. Now you can double or triple the recipe easily by adding more assessments and developing revitalization plans.

Ingredients
    Environmental scan
    Current state assessments
    1 future state vision
    1 mission statement(s)
    Competitive strategy
    Revitalization plans

Makes one serving (for manufacturing or nonmanufacturing)

1. Periodically update the environmental scan, and assess whether the design now in place is still appropriate.
2. Conduct regular assessments between the current state assessment and future state vision.
3. Continue to analyze competitive strategy versus the competition. Simmer.
4. Assess goal performance and relevance of goals to team mission.
5. Establish a vision for the next generation of the change effort.
6. Develop revitalization plans.
7. Celebrate successes.
8. Serve.

Variation
Develop a scenario of the expected future business situation and assess ability to be successful in that future scenario.

Tip
It is important to assess individual and team level empowerment behaviors throughout the change strategy and even more critical as the empowerment design is implemented. Compare to behaviors

that should be present in such a culture, identify areas in need of improvement, and collaborate on actions for correction!

Sample Renewal

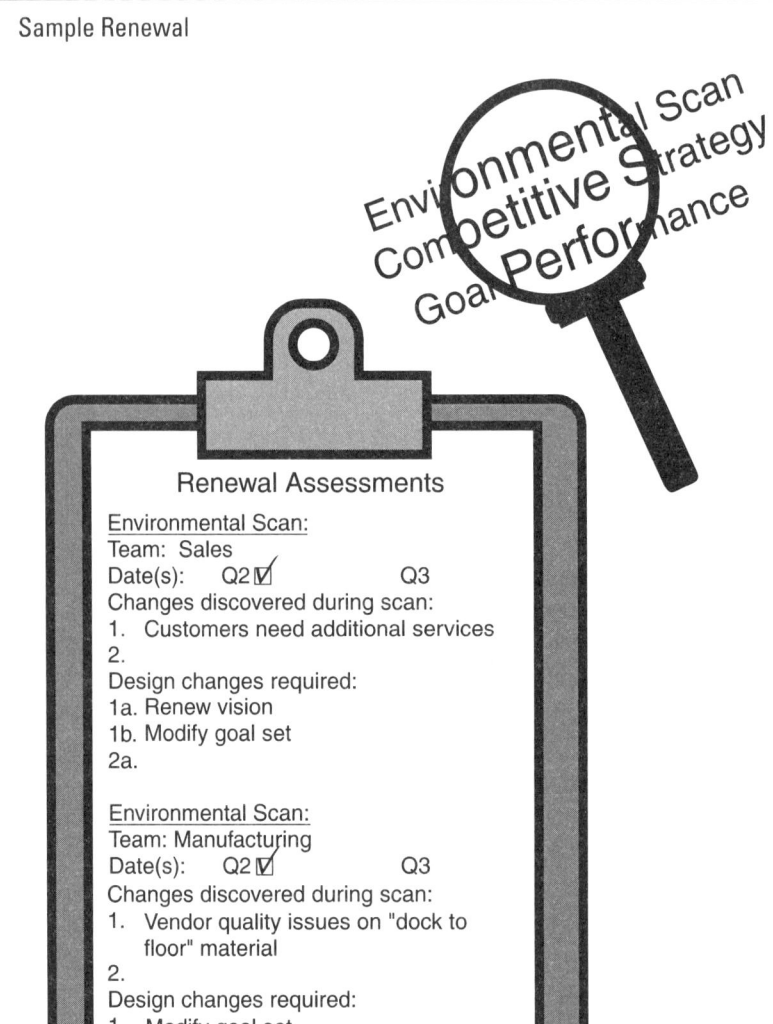

Renewal Assessments

Environmental Scan:
Team: Sales
Date(s):   Q2 ☑   Q3
Changes discovered during scan:
1. Customers need additional services
2.
Design changes required:
1a. Renew vision
1b. Modify goal set
2a.

Environmental Scan:
Team: Manufacturing
Date(s):   Q2 ☑   Q3
Changes discovered during scan:
1. Vendor quality issues on "dock to floor" material
2.
Design changes required:
1. Modify goal set
2.

Empowerment Process Model
Cooked to Perfection Elements

Manufacturing Recipes:

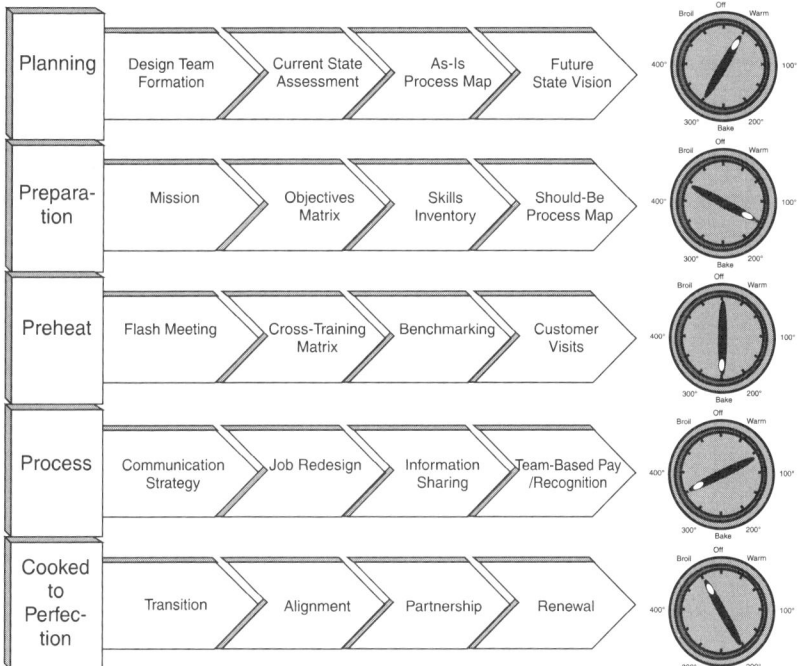

Empowerment Process Model
Cooked to Perfection Elements

Nonmanufacturing Recipes:

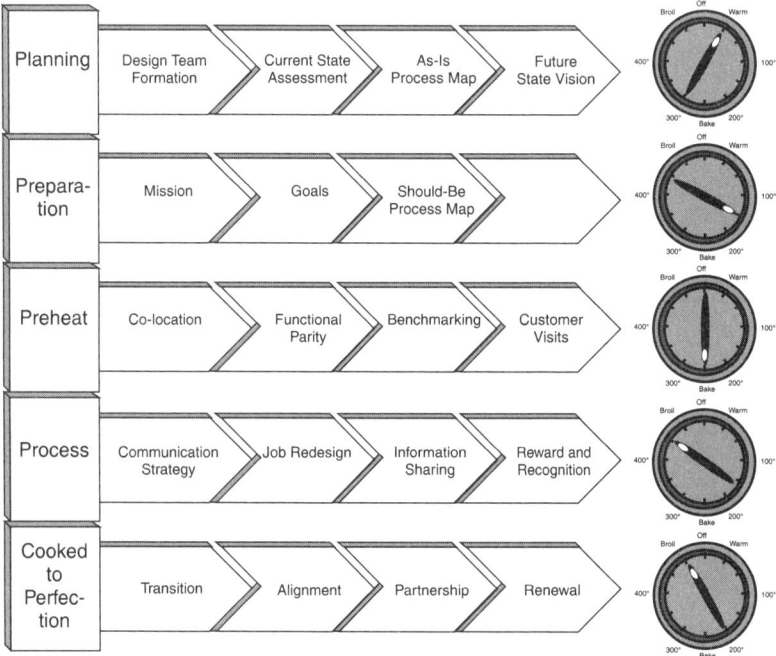

SUMMARY

Empowered teams provide organizations with a capacity to leverage people as a competitive advantage. Your task as Champion of Empowered Organizations was to do just that; you did! The commitment and passion that you demonstrated throughout the empowerment process is a primary reason why the change effort was successful.

The cooked-to-perfection part of the journey is strewn with many obstacles, notably the comfort level that a significant number of people have experienced within the current state. It is within this process stage that design becomes reality, and the transition to the ideal future state completes the last leg of the trek. Involvement, commitment, and support from those who can effect a successful transition will be significant allies; partner with them!

The alignment of organizational systems that run counter to empowered team implementation will cause concern and focus for modification or redesign. New systems may have to be designed that will enhance the capacity for empowerment to succeed. Take the time, elicit help in addressing the issues. A hierarchy of business goals will have to be reviewed and aligned. The business results that the organization desires must be a common thread throughout the structure and a means of measuring that progress be validated.

Finally, renewal will be ever so important in gauging whether the current design is appropriate for realized changes in the environment, in competitive strategy, or in organizational values. The correction process never really ends!

The change strategy is cooking! The temperature of the organization for success is now perfect!

PART SIX

DESSERT

DESSERT

It has been my experience that the finishing touch to any successful empowerment initiative is dessert. Although I don't know for sure where the following recipe came from, I can only suspect that it was passed down from a generation of champions before me. In fact, I had once heard that this dessert would only be made upon the successful implementation of empowered teams. As the story goes, many batches of this particular dessert would be made in the empowerment kitchens of these champions and sampled, as a celebration, by everyone involved in the change effort. The taste of this dessert was said to have such a delightful burst of flavor that it kept the empowerment momentum alive for years to follow. In fact, the story continues, members from those teams began looking for opportunities in other parts of their businesses to launch the empowerment initiative, not only to improve performance and effect a cultural change, but to experience that special taste of success again and again.

Just to let you know, I have had the pleasure of experiencing this taste of success many times during my years as a Champion of Empowered Organizations. I hope that you will be as fortunate as I in experiencing its delightful flavor. There is nothing more satisfying than seeing that joyful look from a successful team when you serve them *empowermints!*

EMPOWERMINTS

For a special touch to the completion of any successful empowerment initiative, whip up a batch of these tantalizing mints. The flavorful burst from each will send you off looking for other empowerment opportunities!

Ingredients

    1 8 oz. package of cream cheese
    1/4 cup soft butter or margarine
    2 1-lb. packages of powdered sugar
    1/2 teaspoon peppermint extract
    Food coloring

Makes multiple servings for (manufacturing or nonmanufacturing)

1. Combine cream cheese and butter in a saucepan and stir over low heat until melted.
2. Add powdered sugar gradually until mixed well.
3. Add peppermint extract and drops of food coloring (any color).
4. Cool. Roll into one-inch balls and place on wax paper.
5. Let stand uncovered overnight.
6. Serve and enjoy!

Variation
Substitute other flavored extracts for peppermint (e.g., lemon, banana, orange). Use any food color variations (yellow, green, orange, red, etc.).

Tip
Place mints in small container and label as empowermints. An empowering dessert for the entrees just served!

Sample Empowermints

EPILOGUE

As Champion of Empowered Organizations, you have every right to stake claim to that title, but your task is not yet complete; the likelihood is that it never will be! As stated earlier, success conditions many organizations to persist in old ways of doing business. Don't fall into that trap! Business survival today requires a constant look forward with an occasional glance backward. Look forward by doing scenario planning and establish a vision for the next generation of the change effort. Glance backward to remind yourself why change was necessary and the extent to which change has been successful. Understand that change is constant; customers, competition, and employees will demand it! As a champion, you now have the experience, the process, and the recipes to respond!

Issues in Implementing Empowered Teams

Building a Compelling Case for Change

Commitment and support for change must start with senior managers. They are a key ingredient in building a compelling case for implementing empowered teams. Framing the impact of change drivers will convince some, but not all, senior level managers that change is necessary. In some cases, senior managers must be convinced, not only of the need for change, but also of the specific change strategy. It can be extremely helpful if you can facilitate dialogue between senior-level advocates of change and those that are not convinced of the need to persuade or to strengthen commitment. Your role as champion is to enlist advocate support in convincing others at that level of the need for change!

Teams understand that commitment and support for change must start at the top. "Does senior management support empowerment?" is assuredly the first question that they will ask. You will need to have an affirmative answer to that question before the journey begins. Teams will want to hear top-level communication of commitment and support. That communication must convince the rest of the organization of the need for change; it could be the difference between success and failure of the change effort. The right message for senior managers to send is to convey the reasons for change and the consequences of not implementing empowered teams.

Another critical element in building a case for change is middle manager commitment. The same message that senior management sends must be shared and communicated by middle managers. As a champion, you may have to clarify their role in the change effort and the importance of a consistent message.

Finally, union leadership is another group for whom commitment and support of change will be critical. They will have to be convinced of the benefits that will be realized by their members. Educating union leadership on the benefits and outcomes that an empowered team structure will bring will be another important task for you as champion.

One last word of caution! It has been my experience that quite often, both senior and/or middle managers will have expectations of short-term results. Impatience with the pace of change coupled with a lack of short-term results may be a difficult hurdle to overcome. Therefore, set realistic expectations of results, and a realistic time frame for process completion, and reinforce outcomes of the change process. Constant dialogue throughout the empowerment process will be essential for maintaining management focus.

Building a compelling case for change will require the commitment and support of senior and middle management, as well as of union leadership. Educating these key stakeholders on the benefits, outcomes, and processes of implementing empowered teams will be critical to forming a partnership for the change effort. Successful implementation will depend on a strong alliance and cohesive support for a change process that may take a significant amount of time to complete. The rest of the organization will be listening for their "voice" and "watching" their actions as the journey unfolds.

Pace versus Process Time

Empowerment is not an overnight fix; it is a process! In fact, it may take several years for teams to evolve along the empowerment continuum. As a champion, know that you probably will not be in a position to set the pace of the change effort to match your expectation or need; but you can be influential. Engaging teams into the empowerment process is done outside the scope of individual and team work assignments. Time spent on the change effort will more than likely be a compromise among team members and management as to the amount of time per week or per month to spend on change activities. Try to avoid a directive; remember, this is an empowering process!

The question of how long it will take a team to go through the empowerment process will be asked frequently; the answer will depend on many variables, such as: the scope of the team vision and mission, the gap between the current and ideal future state, the willingness of the organization to allow changes to be implemented, and the amount of time that teams commit to the change effort. And these are just a few of the key variables. As stated earlier, it has been my experience that the range of time needed to evolve through the empowerment process will take between 15 months and five years. Certainly, the more time that is devoted to the change effort, the greater the pace, and the less time for process completion.

As a guideline, the majority of teams that I have championed spend two to four hours per week on empowerment process activities in some combination of group meetings and off-line tasks. For certain recipes of this process model it may be appropriate to spend larger blocks of time to accelerate the outcome or to allow for continuity of design or action. Both you and the team will be able to gauge the need for when additional time is required.

As champion, influence teams to maximize the amount of time that they can spend on the change process. Provided that there has been a consistent message from management and unions relative to the need for change and their support, you should be able to make a compelling case for team commitment, as well. Let everyone know at the outset the context of the process model to be used, the anticipated benefits and outcomes, and the pace of change versus process of change.

Champions/Facilitators

Senior managers can demonstrate their commitment to empowered teams by dedicating resources to the change effort (time, people, and money). Because team members generally lack experience in group process, trained or certified champions/facilitators are critical in planning strategy and providing direction. Unfortunately, not having this role staffed with the appropriate expertise may be a by-product of the lack of commitment by senior managers.

There are really two types of internal champions, self-designated and those who are either asked or assigned by the organization. Self-designated champions are generally in a position of responsibility for team performance and do so from a vision of greater opportunity for performance improvement. However, self-designated champions usually find themselves without a broad brush of organizational support and with limited personal time and experience in driving a change strategy. Management and peers, in most cases, will be skeptical of any success attributed to the empowerment process and can undermine the change effort very easily. Subsequently, the task for this type of champion can be monumental in convincing management of empowerment-related successes and in engaging more teams into this change process. That is not to say that teams with this kind of champion can't be successful, but they may very well be an island of success within the larger framework of the organization and not receive the recognition that they deserve.

If you are a self-designated champion, the change effort may well rest on your shoulders alone. Failure may make you more visible and vulnerable than any success would. My recommendation is to highlight successes, large or small, tied to performance improvement and keep selling the empowerment process at every opportunity to the rest of the organization.

In my experience, organizations that dedicate staffing to the role of a champion/facilitator will have a greater success rate than those that do not. With organizational commitment and support, the change effort becomes more of a partnership in success or failure. Full-time dedicated champions will have the time to work the issues or obstacles that teams may encounter, and be the team's voice with succeeding levels of management. A full-time champion can keep teams on the right course. I have had the experience of being in both roles; each is rewarding, but the latter is optimal!

Legal

One of the most common mistakes made during the empowered-team design process is not engaging legal counsel to provide guidance concerning the boundaries within which teams can operate. Consistent with a company's code of conduct, each empowered team must comply with the laws of the country in which it operates and with applicable company policies and procedures. Involving legal counsel early in the planning stage of the empowerment process model will create an awareness of limits that design actions can't exceed. Beyond the planning stage, it would be beneficial for legal representation to conduct periodic reviews of team participation in all stages of the empowerment process to be able to address any developing issues in various legal arenas.

The operating principles that govern empowered teams should be formulated, documented, and communicated to teams upon formation. They can be framed by senior management and legal counsel either with or without the collaboration of the empowered teams. It is my opinion that collaboration is more effective for reasons of participation and dialogue regarding the rationale and acceptance for inclusion in such a list. Subject matter coverage of operating principles should include anything that could infringe upon compliance with the laws of the country in which empowered teams operate, as well as company policy and procedures. A good starting point is to state the reasons for the existence of empowered teams!

Realize that as teams evolve along the empowerment continuum, they will continue to test organizational boundaries and the limits of applicable company policies and procedures. They will do so from an increasing capacity and desire to take ownership for a whole product, process, and/or service. As a champion, you will be encouraged by the enthusiasm, progress, and momentum of teams to change the status quo, but always remember that there are limits; involve legal early and often!

Organized Labor

In some organizations, organized labor is crucial to the change effort. Unions can be unfamiliar with empowered teams and the benefits that can be realized by its members. Unions, like management, not only face the same external competitive pressures but also the changing values of today's workforce. Educating union leadership and management on the empowerment process can be a significant task. Yet, teams that are developed and implemented in a collaboration between organized labor and management can provide a solid foundation for future change.

The Future

It is my opinion that empowered teams will be the primary building blocks of company performance for the future. The performance potential of these teams is the key to improving performance in all types of organizations, regardless of size, product, or service. Without them, I would argue, we cannot meet the significant competitive challenges that lie ahead.

While some organizations are leading-edge, others are moving forward very cautiously, while still others are being dragged into the future by competitors, customers, or innovation. Regardless, it is inevitable that most organizations will look to empowered teams as a breakthrough opportunity to improve performance and deliver results. The competitive edge will belong to those organizations that capitalize on the potential of these resources.

Empowered-team applications will continue to extend well beyond manufacturing, where a recent history of successful transitions has been documented. A greater use of empowered teams will continue to surface in the white collar ranks. As competitive pressures escalate, the need for organizations to continue to transform themselves will be critical and necessary. Empowerment as a proven change strategy will capture the attention of those in leadership roles and provide the capacity to leverage increasing employee involvement. Change agents will be essential!

Chefs of Empowered Organizations

My journey as a change agent for a major global corporation began without the benefit of experience or guidance. It is likely that many of you will take the same path. Some of you will navigate the road to empowerment successfully, others will not. Regardless of the road that your journey takes, I hope that you dedicate yourself to bringing a vision into reality with passion and purpose. It is your character and will that drives you to succeed. It is the stuff that champions are made of!

It was my vision that this book would provide you with a process and recipes for making a successful transition to empowered teams. As you make that transition and your organization is cooked to perfection, you will join those many others who have tasted success as Champions of Empowered Organizations. Or maybe we should say as Chefs of Empowered Organizations!

INDEX

Alignment, 97, 101–103
As-is process maps, 3–4
  developing, 17–18
  job redesign and, 78
  should-be process maps and, 41
  skills inventory and, 35
  transition stage, 99

Benchmarking, 49, 63–64, 70
Bicknell, Barbara A., 65
Bicknell, Kris D., 65
Boyett, Joseph H., 83

Champions of Empowered Organizations (CEOs), 123
  versus facilitators, 120–121
  planning responsibilities, 24
  preheat stage tasks, 70
  tasks, 111
Change
  elements for building case for, 118–119
  strategy for, 70
Change drivers, xvii–xviii
Collaboration, 97
Co-location, 49, 59–60
Communication strategy, 73, 75–77, 92
Compensation programs, 73, 83–86, 92
Complaint letters, 65
Conn, Henry P., 83
Cover letters, 5, 7–8
Cross-training matrix, 49, 55–58
Current state assessments, 3, 5–9
  renewal, 107
  transition stage, 99
Customer sensitivity, 65
Customer visits, 49, 65–67

Design teams, 3, 35
  formation of, 10–12

Design teams *continued*
  sample, 13
Development Dimensions International, 5
Dialogue, 70
Disconnects, 17, 19
Distribution lists, 5, 9

Empowered teams
  definition, xvi–xvii
  issues in implementing, 118–123
  results of, xxi
  versus traditional, xvii
Empowerment, 97
  continuum/process, xviii–xx
  definition, xv–xvi
  pace versus process time, 119–120
  planning, 3–4
  results from, xxi
Empowerment process model
  cooked to perfection elements, 109–110
  planning element, 22–24
  preheat elements, 68–69
  preparation element, 43–44
  process elements, 90–91
Empowermints, recipe, 116
Environmental scan, 3, 11, 14–15, 107–109

Flash meetings, 49, 51–54
Focus groups, 65, 97
Functional parity, 49, 61–62
Future state vision, 20–21, 78
  renewal, 107
  transition, 99

Gap analysis, 19; *See also* Disconnects
Goals, 38–40
High-performance work teams; *See* Empowered teams

Index

Improvement targets, 30
Information sharing, 73, 81–82, 92, 105
Job assignment, 101–103
Job redesign, 73, 78–80, 92
Labor relations, 101–103, 119, 122–123
Legal counsel, use of, 121–122

Manufacturing organizations
  alignment, 101–103
  benchmarking, 63–64
  communication strategy, 75–77
  compensation programs, 83–86
  creating vision, 20–21
  cross-training matrix, 55–58
  customer visits, 65–67
  design teams, 10–16
  flash meetings, 51–54
  information sharing, 81–82
  job redesign, 78–80
  partnership, 104–106
  process maps, 17–19
  should-be process maps, 41–42
  skills inventory, 27, 35–37
  transition stage, 99–100
Mission statement(s)
  job redesign and, 78
  objectives matrix and, 30
  planning stage and, 27, 28–29
  renewal stage and, 107
  skills inventory and, 35

Nonmanufacturing organizations
  alignment, 101–103
  benchmarking, 63–64
  co-location, 59–60
  communication strategy, 75–77
  creating vision, 20–21
  customer visits, 65–67
  design teams, 10–16
  functional parity, 61–62
  goals, 38–40
  information sharing, 81–82
  job redesign, 78–80
  partnership, 104–106
  process maps, 17–19
  reward and recognition programs, 87–89

Nonmanufacturing organizations *continued*
  should-be process maps, 41–42
  skills inventory, 27
  transition stage, 99–100

Objectives matrix, 27, 30–34
Organizations, traditional versus empowered team, xvii
Organized labor, 122–123
Partnership, 104–106
Partnerships, 97
Performance measurement, 83–86, 92–93
Process maps
  as-is, 3–4, 17–18, 42, 78, 99
  should-be, 27, 41–42, 78, 99
Quality functional deployment (QFD), 65

Recognition programs, 83–86, 87–89, 93
Renewal, 97, 107–109
Revitalization plans, 97
Rewards, 87–89, 93
Roadmaps, 38, 99
Scenario planning, 118
Should-be process maps, 27, 41–42
  job redesign stage and, 78
  transition stage, 99
Skills inventory, 27, 35–37
Sponsors, 3
Sponsorship matrix, 16

Team-based pay, 83–86
Team performance evaluation, 32–34
Teamwork, 92
The Roadmap to Repeatable Success, Using QFD to Implement Change, 65
Transition stage, 97, 99–100
Unions, 10–11, 122–123
Vision, 28, 35, 118
Vision, creation of, 4
Vision, formation of, 20–21
Voice-of-the customer tools, 65
Workplace 2000, 83
Zenger-Miller, Inc., 5